Lost Masterpieces

Lost
Masterpieces

Michael Collins

Produced for DK by Toucan Books

DK LONDON
Senior Editor Scarlett O'Hara
Senior Designer Mark Cavanagh
Managing Editor Gareth Jones
Senior Managing Art Editor Lee Griffiths
Senior Production Editor Gillian Reid
Senior Production Controller Rachel Ng
Illustrator Emma Fraser Reid
Jacket Design Development Manager
Sophia M.T.T.
Jacket Designer Akiko Kato
Associate Publishing Director Liz Wheeler
Art Director Karen Self
Publishing Director Jonathan Metcalf

DK DELHI
Senior Jackets Designer: Suhita Dharamjit
Senior DTP Designer: Harish Aggarwal
Senior Jackets Coordinator: Priyanka Sharma-Saddi

First published in Great Britain in 2022 by
Dorling Kindersley Limited
DK, One Embassy Gardens, 8 Viaduct Gardens,
London, SW11 7BW

Copyright © 2022 Dorling Kindersley Limited
A Penguin Random House Company
10 9 8 7 6 5 4 3 2 1
001–326802–June/2022

All rights reserved.
No part of this publication may be
reproduced, stored in or introduced into a
retrieval system, or transmitted, in any form,
or by any means (electronic, mechanical,
photocopying, recording, or otherwise),
without the prior written permission of
the copyright owner.

A CIP catalogue record for this book
is available from the British Library.
ISBN: 978-0-2415-3639-1

Printed and bound in Latvia

For the curious
www.dk.com

FSC
www.fsc.org
MIX
Paper | Supporting
responsible forestry
FSC™ C018179

This book was made with Forest
Stewardship Council™ certified
paper – one small step in DK's
commitment to a sustainable future.
For more information go to
www.dk.com/our-green-pledge

Contents

6   Introduction

Lost

10   The Tomb of King Tutankhamun
14   Aphrodite of Knidos
16   The Terracotta Army
18   The Alexander Mosaic
20   China's Guardian Beasts
22   The Tabula Rogeriana
24   Salvator Mundi
28   Fondaco dei Tedeschi
29   The Sistine Tapestries
30   Lucretia
32   Zodiac Fountain Water Clock
34   Anna Feodorovna
36   The Death of Cleopatra
38   Modern Woman
40   The Battle of San Jacinto
41   Red and Green II
42   Reclining Nude
44   December in Venice
46   The Reaper
48   The Wounded Table
50   Struggle: From the History
     of the American People
52   Life's Work
54   Untitled Gouache
55   The Lenin Mosaic
56   Touching North

Stolen

60   Mexican Antiquities
61   The Book of Kells
62   The Ghent Altarpiece
64   The Last Judgement
66   Mona Lisa
68   St Christopher Carrying the
     Christ Child

70 The Benin Bronzes
74 Nativity with St Francis and
   St Lawrence
76 The Head of a Bearded Man
78 Adam and Eve
80 The Isabella Stewart Gardner Heist
84 Lioness and Lion in a Cave
86 Les Choristes
88 Funerary Pole
90 Summer's Day
92 View of the Sea at Scheveningen
94 The Gates of Hell
96 The Scream
98 Portraits of Adele
100 Swamp Legend
104 Reading Girl in White and Yellow
105 Myrto
106 Portrait of Francis Bacon
107 Two Forms (Divided Circle)
108 Wine of Babylon
109 Camouflage Series
110 Chloe & Emma

Damaged

114 Nineveh's Lamassu
118 Parthenon Marbles
120 The Portland Vase
121 Sutton Hoo Helmet
122 Statue of Vishnu
124 The Bayeux Tapestry
126 Frescoes of the Lives of St Francis
   and the Saints
128 Pietà
132 The Night Watch
134 The Rokeby Venus
136 The Dream
138 Yellow Pumpkin
140 Niagara Falls

Destroyed

144 The Buddhas of Bamiyan
146 The Justice of Trajan and
   Herkinbald
148 Bonfire of the Vanities
150 Equestrian Portrait of Emperor
   Philip IV
154 The Amber Room
156 The Last Moments of Michel
   Lepeletier
158 Religion Attended by the Virtues
160 The Stone Breakers
162 Washington Crossing the
   Delaware
164 Beneath the Blue Room
166 Water Lilies
168 Man at the Crossroads
170 Three Works
172 Lift Every Voice and Sing
   (The Harp)
174 Portrait of Winston Churchill
176 Figurative Work
177 Reclining Figure
178 Everyone I Have Ever Slept With
182 Dropping a Han Dynasty Urn
184 Pillar of Shame
186 Love is in the Bin

188 Index
192 Acknowledgments

Introduction

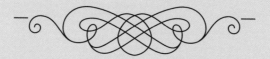

For thousands of years, we have embellished the world with art, creating a vast treasury using stone, wood, metal, pigments, and other materials. The urge to create art is one of the fundamental impulses of humanity.

It is impossible to know how much art has been created, let alone how much of this has disappeared. This book takes the reader on an intriguing trail across the globe in search of art that we know has been plundered, damaged, stolen, deliberately destroyed, or simply lost, its fate undocumented. Spanning some five millennia, it provides a glimpse of the vanished achievements of ancient artisans, Old Masters, Modernists and Post-Modernists, and some of the avant-garde artists of today.

Art theft from museums and private collections is a highly lucrative crime, netting billions of dollars every year. There is also a brisk trade in forgeries, with half of the artworks offered for sale each year believed to be fakes. From time to time, works of art are found, usually through the work of dogged art detectives but sometimes purely by chance. In 2017, *Les Choristes*, a work by French Impressionist painter Edgar Degas that had been stolen nine years earlier, was found in the luggage compartment of a bus. Such finds are rare, but we continue to hope that some of the lost masterpieces of the world will be discovered, bringing joy and inspiration to all who see them.

Lost

The Tomb of King Tutankhamun

❖ c. 1325 BCE

I n November 1922, the British archaeologist Howard Carter discovered the burial chamber of the then little-known boy-pharaoh Tutankhamun, who had died in 1323 BCE. Carter had spent several seasons excavating the barren area of Egypt's Valley of the Kings. The chance discovery of a staircase led him down a flight of 16 steps to a sealed doorway. At this point, he dispatched a telegram to his patron Lord Carnarvon in England, who immediately set sail for Egypt. On 26 November, in the presence of Carnarvon, Carter broke through two doors, having noted that the doors had been resealed twice in antiquity. Fearing that the tomb had already been plundered, he peered into the chamber with only a taper to see by. To his astonishment, he saw "everywhere the glint of gold".

Although ancient tomb-robbers may have got into the entrance corridor, it appeared that the tomb itself had remained intact, its door hidden behind an accumulation of rubble. The tomb contained more than 5,000 objects, including four chariots, a set of three coffins inside

" At last have made wonderful discovery in valley; a magnificent tomb with seals intact: recovered same for your arrival; congratulations. "

Howard Carter, telegram to Lord Carnarvon, 1922

a stone sarcophagus, and a solid gold mask covering the king's face, along with statues, furniture, gilt carvings, lamps, and jewellery – all of which had lain undisturbed for 3,000 years.

Tutankhamun was 18 when he died. Archaeologists have speculated that the young king's death may have been unexpected, and the burial preparations therefore rushed. The tomb is small for a pharaoh, and his successor may have arranged for him to be buried in a tomb that already existed rather than one that was tailor-made.

Howard Carter examines the sarcophagus of Tutankhamun, c. 1925.

The gold mask of Tutankhamun

" Details of the room within
emerged slowly from the mist,
strange animals, statues and gold –
everywhere the glint of gold. "

Howard Carter, 1922

A team of archaeologists joined Carter to help map, measure, and photograph the tomb's contents, which had to be done before the items were removed and handed over to the Egyptian state. The task of emptying the tomb and cataloguing its items took almost a decade. Years later, it materialized that Carter had not been as scrupulous in this endeavour as he pretended. Artefacts in several museums, including the Metropolitan Museum of Art, in New York, were shown to have come from Tutankhamun's tomb. The Met returned these items to Egypt in 2011.

Almost a century after the tomb's discovery, the stone chambers showed signs of disintegration. Humidity and airborne pollutants introduced by hundreds of thousands of visitors had caused parts of the wall paintings to flake off. Some visitors had even removed tiny fragments as souvenirs. The tomb was closed to the public and a replica for tourists to visit was created about 2.5 km (1.5 miles) away in order to preserve the original. While doing research for the replica, technicians making ultrasound scans of the tomb's walls identified two areas that may contain further chambers.

The Grand Egyptian Museum near the pyramids at Giza provides a state-of-the-art showcase for the treasures of ancient Egypt. Almost all the items known to have come from Tutankhamun's tomb have been reunited here for the first time since 1922. The one item that remains in the tomb is the mummy of the boy-pharaoh, kept in a climate-controlled glass case.

Book of the Dead

Most of the important text known as The Book of the Dead is missing from Tutankhamun's treasures. A series of spells and invocations composed over several centuries by priests and scribes, the text was placed in tombs to accompany the body into the afterlife. It enabled the deceased to present their heart, the seat of the intellect, will, and memory, to the gods for judgement. The gods weighed the heart against the feather of truth.

Aphrodite
of Knidos

c.350 BCE

" Its shrine is completely open, so that it is possible to observe the goddess from every side; she herself, it is believed, favoured it being made that way. "

Pliny the Elder, first century CE

In July 1969, the American archaeologist Iris Cornelia Love announced that she had uncovered the remains of the Temple of Knidos on the southwest coast of Turkey. This ancient sanctuary had contained one of the earliest representations of Aphrodite, the Greek goddess of love. Carved from white marble by the sculptor Praxiteles in the fourth century BCE, the statue was the first recorded example of a life-size representation of a nude woman. The statue enjoyed great fame. Sailors would have visited the temple to entreat the goddess to grant them a safe passage across the ocean.

The temple was probably destroyed in the fifth century, following Roman emperor Theodosius I's decree that pagan temples should be closed or converted into churches. Love claimed that the statue of Aphrodite had stood on the damaged pedestal at the centre of the circular temple ruins. She had found marble fragments, including pieces of an oversized hand, lying nearby, together with votive offerings.

Love maintained that the head of the original statue was in the British Museum, a claim she made in 1970 after reviewing the museum's unexhibited items from Knidos and coming across a crumbling marble head in the museum's basement. The museum strenuously denied the claim, and it is impossible to know if the fragments found by Love were part of the original statue. While the original might be lost, several copies from the Roman era remain, allowing us to imagine what the goddess might have looked like.

The Kaufmann head (150 BCE), in the Louvre, is thought to be a copy of the head of Aphrodite at Knidos.

Terracotta Army

246–210 BCE

On 29 March 1974, farmers digging a well near the city of Xi'an, in northwest China, unearthed several pieces of terracotta and some bronze arrowheads. The find occurred near the tomb of the first Chinese emperor, Qin Shi Huang (ruled 221–210 BCE). A local museum curator pieced together the fragments, producing two 1.78 m- (5 ft 10 in-) high warrior figures.

Over the next 40 years, archaeologists excavated around 2,000 life-size terracotta soldiers of different ranks, with distinct features, clothes, and hairstyles, 130 chariots drawn by 520 horses, and 150 cavalry horses, all buried in long pits and intended to protect the emperor in the afterlife. Smaller pits contained figures of court officials, acrobats, musicians, and exotic animals and birds, each one, like the warriors, individually fashioned.

The emperor had ordered the construction of his mausoleum in 246 BCE, soon after he became emperor at the age of 13. Not long after his death, raiders looted the figures and set fire to the pits. The ceilings collapsed, toppling and smashing many of the terracotta figures, and the pits filled up with earth. Hidden in the ground, the figures lay undisturbed for around 2,200 years, lost to human knowledge.

The total number of statues is estimated to be about 8,000, and originally the figures were painted in bright colours and lacquered. As the archaeologists extracted the pieces from the ground, however, they quickly noticed that the colours faded within minutes. Exposed to the air, the lacquer, which had been preserved by the moisture in the soil, dried out and cracked into thousands of fragments.

Archaeologists continue to make discoveries in the area. New techniques are used to protect the colour, such as dipping the pieces in a solution that bonds the lacquer to the terracotta surface. The emperor's tomb remains sealed in order to protect the contents.

" I saw seven or eight pieces – bits of legs, arms, and two heads – lying near the well, along with some bricks. "

Zhao Kangmin, archaeologist, 2007

Infantry figures, including two generals (at the back) wearing crowns

The Alexander Mosaic

100 BCE

" We of Macedon for generations past have been trained in the hard school of danger and war. "

Alexander the Great, 333 BCE

The mosaic depicts Darius turning in his chariot to look at Alexander.

In 1831, archaeologists excavating a villa known as the House of the Faun in the Roman city of Pompeii unearthed a large floor mosaic that had been buried for more than 1,700 years. The eruption of Mount Vesuvius in 79 CE may have destroyed the city, but the deep layer of ash and mud preserved many of its frescoes and mosaics.

The mosaic captures the turning point in the Battle of Issus in 333 BCE between Greek forces led by the Macedonian prince Alexander the Great, the ultimate victor, and the army of the Persian Empire under King Darius III. Alexander, on horseback, charges towards Darius, who turns in his chariot to look back at the impudent youth. Measuring 2.72 m by 5.13 m (8 ft 11 in by 16 ft 10 in), the mosaic was made from more than one and a half million tesserae – small, square-cut pieces of coloured tiles and glass.

The mosaic was removed from Pompeii in 1843 and transferred to the National Archaeological Museum in Naples. In 2003, a team from the International Centre for the Study and Teaching of Mosaic in Ravenna made a copy of it and installed it in the mosaic's original location in the House of the Faun.

China's Guardian Beasts

◦————◇————◦

c. 800 CE

In 1908, an American scientific expedition in the Chinese province of Gansu came across an intact, eighth-century tomb. Inside was a pair of fearsome-looking ceramic figures, part-animal and part-human. They sat in front of the coffin, placed there to provide the dead with a safe journey into the afterlife and ward off tomb-raiders. Wealthy people packed their tombs with objects that they might need after death, and these guardian beasts, or *zhenmoushou*, were common.

Zhenmoushou were highly popular during the Tang Dynasty. The pair discovered in Gansu are earthenware figures that were originally brightly painted and gilded. One has the head of a lion, the other of a man. They have scowling faces and clawed feet, their heads are surrounded by tongues of fire, and they sit ready to spring.

Regardless of the guardian beasts' fierce appearance, thieves regularly succeeded in raiding tombs, and sometimes even carried away these protectors of the dead. For centuries, small farmers were the real guardians of the tombs that lay beneath their land. During the latter part of the 20th century though, many farmers moved to the cities, making it easier for robbers to dig for antiquities worth billions of pounds.

Tomb-raiding continues to be a vast illegal industry in China, with tens of thousands of tombs vandalized each year. Well-organized criminals employ increasingly sophisticated means to identify hidden tombs and supply an ever-growing illegal art market across the world. In 2017, a court in Beijing condemned tomb-robber Yao Yuzhong to death for his three-decades career. The sentence was later commuted to a term in prison.

" The flamboyantly sculpted *zhenmoushou* looked out from their places in front of the coffin to ward off evil. **"**

Clark Art Institute, Williamstown, Massachusetts

The Tabula Rogeriana

Muhammad al-Idrisi

1154

In 1138, Arab scholar, geographer, and cartographer Muhammad al-Idrisi entered the employment of Roger II, King of Sicily. Al-Idrisi had travelled extensively, and Roger commissioned him to write a description of the population centres of the entire known world.

Al-Idrisi began his work by studying the writings of Arabian mariners and the Alexandrian historian Ptolemy. For some 15 years, he interviewed sailors and merchants in order to learn from their travels. Working alongside other scholars appointed by Roger, he pieced together an atlas of the known world. The scholars also prepared maps to accompany the text.

When Roger received al-Idrisi's *Nuzhat al-Mushtak*, known in the West as the *Tabula Rogeriana*, he commissioned artisans to incise a map of the world on a circular silver disc measuring 200 cm (80 in) in diameter and weighing around 135 kg (300 lb). South appeared at the top of the disc and north at the bottom, with Mecca at the centre. According to al-Idrisi's calculations, the Earth's circumference measured about 36,855 km (22,900 miles), a measurement that has proved remarkably accurate (it is actually 40,075 km/24,900 miles).

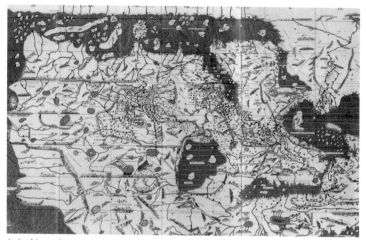

As in this modern reconstruction, the *Tabula Rogeriana* orientated north at the bottom.

The original copy of al-Idrisi's atlas and the disc disappeared from the historical record shortly after Roger's death in 1154. However, several copies of the book were made, some of which survive. In 2018, a replica disc based on al-Idrisi's maps was displayed at the Bodleian Library in Oxford, England, which has a 16th-century copy of the atlas that it had bought in 1692. Another copy of the book is kept in Palermo, where al-Idrisi had prepared the original.

" [Roger] wished that he should
accurately know the details
of his land and master them
with a definite knowledge. "

Muhammad al-Idrisi

Salvator Mundi

❦

Leonardo da Vinci

1500

Salvator Mundi by Leonardo da Vinci

An oil painting on a walnut wood panel, titled *Salvator Mundi* (Saviour of the World) and attributed to Leonardo da Vinci, sold at Christie's in New York in 2017 for $450.3 million. It was the highest price ever achieved by a painting at public auction. The portrait of Christ with one hand held up in blessing and the other holding a crystal sphere was scheduled to be unveiled at the Louvre Abu Dhabi in 2018, but was withdrawn at the last moment. Denounced as a fake by some art experts, it has disappeared from public view.

The challenge for art scholars is to trace a direct line, or provenance, from the artist to the present day. For the *Salvator Mundi* sold at Christie's, there is no clear provenance.

No artist of the Renaissance period could afford to begin a work without a contract, because materials such as pigments were expensive. If there ever was a contract between Leonardo da Vinci and a patron for this subject, it has not survived. To complicate

" [If] you look at Leonardo's curls, or how he handles twisted drapery, he understands the physics of it. He understands the anatomy of the phenomenon. "

Martin Kemp, Leonardo scholar, 2018

matters, some 20 versions of the *Salvator Mundi* exist, but no one has been able to identify definitively which is the original and which are the copies.

Leonardo was well aware of his extraordinary abilities. Writing to the Duke of Milan in the late 15th century, the 30-year-old artist listed his talents in design, notably bridges, canals, canons, armoured vehicles, and architecture. Only at the end did he add "Likewise, in painting, I can do everything possible". It was no understatement. Leonardo painted *The Last Supper* and the *Mona Lisa* (see pages 66–67), two of the most iconic works in the history of art. He also developed a particular style called *sfumato*, a blurring of the edges and softening of contours, which became the hallmark of his style.

In 2005, a painting resembling the *Salvator Mundi* turned up at a New Orleans auction house. It was in poor condition, and had clearly suffered from many attempts at restoration. At the time, it was thought to be by Giovanni Boltraffio, a follower of Leonardo da Vinci. Working on a hunch that the painting might come from the hand of Leonardo, the new owners decided to have the panel cleaned and restored. While the cleaning failed to reveal a signature or any other means of verifying the work, exquisite brushwork, which had been hidden under centuries of grime and varnish, emerged. Whoever the mysterious artist was, their skill was undeniable.

The National Gallery in London accepted the painting as an original by Leonardo and exhibited it in 2011. A few years later, a Swiss art dealer sold it to a Russian businessman, who paid

Experiments with light

Leonardo da Vinci was fascinated by light and filled notebooks with his observations on refraction and reflections. Scholars long wondered why the orb held by Christ in the *Salvator Mundi* refracted light incorrectly. It seemed unlikely that Leonardo would make such a mistake. But they were assuming that the orb was solid. In 2020, computer scientists from the University of California, Irvine, proposed that the orb was made from blown glass and therefore hollow, which would cause minimal distortion. They backed up their theory with computer-generated 3-D models. This is one of the puzzles about the painting explained.

$127.5 million. In November 2017, he sold it to Saudi Arabia's Crown Prince Mohammed bin Salma at Christie's auction house in New York for the record-breaking sum of $450.3 million. Mystery continues to surround the painting's whereabouts. There are claims that it might be on a private yacht, or stored in a free port in Switzerland. However, despite much speculation in the world's press and claims about the painting's location, art lovers have yet to see the painting that was last on view at Christie's in 2017.

" Old pictures have to look old – if you take out every crack, every spot, every anomaly, they can easily look like a reproduction. "

Dianne Modestini, conservator, 2011

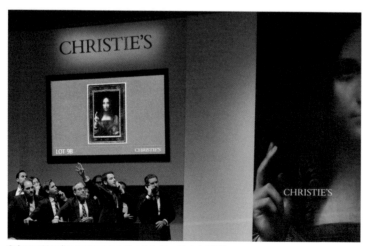

Salvator Mundi is auctioned at Christie's, New York, in 2017.

Fondaco dei Tedeschi

◆———◆———◆

Giorgione and Titian

1508

LOST

In 1508, two young Venetian artists Giorgione and Titian completed a series of frescoes on the exterior of Venice's Fondaco dei Tedeschi. Not long after this, the Venetian air began to eat away at the frescoes' mythological figures, eventually robbing the city of early works by two of its greatest artists.

Founded in 1228, the Fondaco dei Tedeschi was a warehouse on the Grand Canal used for storage and lodging by northern European merchants. In 1505, the building was almost completely destroyed by fire. The Venetian Senate approved its immediate rebuilding, and within three years it was once more open for business. Giorgione and Titian were commissioned to decorate the spaces between the windows – Giorgione on the facade overlooking the Grand Canal, and Titian on a side wall.

In the Venetian tradition, Giorgione and Titian executed the frescoes using bright colours, but these did not remain vivid for long. The sirocco – a hot wind from North Africa laden with salt from the sea – stripped out the pigments. Damp rising from the waters of the lagoon also contributed to the fading of the colours and caused the plaster beneath the frescoes to peel. Damage was also hastened by pollution.

In the 20th century, the remaining fragments were detached from the walls of the building and placed in the Accademia Gallery and the Ca' d'Oro, a former palace on the Grand Canal that is now a museum. They comprise the upper part of a female nude figure by Giorgione and small sections of four frescoes by Titian – *Allegory*, *Justice*, *The Battle Between the Putto and the Dragon*, and *The Battle between Giants and Monsters*. The subjects of the other scenes are entirely lost.

The Sistine Tapestries

Raphael

1516

I n 1515, Pope Leo X, a member of the wealthy Medici banking family, commissioned the painter Raphael to produce designs (called cartoons) for 16 tapestries illustrating the Acts of the Apostles for the Vatican's Sistine Chapel. Raphael and his workshop produced 16 cartoons, which were sent to the atelier of Pieter van Aelst in Brussels. The tapestries were woven in wool and silk, with highlights picked out in gold and silver thread. The first arrived in Rome in late 1519, but Raphael never saw the complete set as he died a few months later.

The tapestries had a chequered history. Several were pawned (later redeemed) to pay for Leo X's funeral expenses in 1521, and they were stolen by troops of the Holy Roman Empire during the Sack of Rome in 1527. Although the tapestries were later returned, they were stolen again, by Napoleon's troops, in 1798.

Ten of the original 16 tapestries survive. The other six may have been destroyed when looters tried to extract the valuable gold thread. Vatican restorers have recreated the missing parts of the tapestries to make a complete set. In February 2020, the tapestries were hung in their original home in the Sistine Chapel for one week to mark the 500th anniversary of Raphael's death.

Lucretia

⟜———◆———⟞

Artemisia Gentileschi

c. 1627

For three centuries, Artemisia Gentileschi, a successful artist in her time, was eclipsed by her father, the painter Orazio Gentileschi, in whose workshop she trained. Her style went out of fashion, and her work was lost to private collections. Yet in 2019, her painting *Lucretia*, capturing the moment before a Roman noblewoman stabs herself after being raped by the royal prince Sextus Tarquinius, emerged from a private collection in France and sold for $5.3 million. The buyer gave the painting to the J. Paul Getty Museum in California.

At the age of 17, Artemisia's career was almost destroyed when she was raped by her tutor, Agostino Tassi. Her father insisted that Tassi marry his daughter, and when Tassi refused (he was already married) and denied the assault, the case went to court. Artemisia was tortured with thumbscrews to test the truth of her allegation, and Tassi was found guilty, but his punishment of exile was never enforced.

In the wake of the court case, Artemisia's reputation was ruined. But she moved from Rome to Florence and then Naples, and went on to build a successful career, becoming the first woman to be admitted

" My illustrious lordship,
I'll show you
what a woman can do. **"**

Artemisia Gentileschi, 1649

to the prestigious Academy of Design in Florence. Her career spanned four decades, but many paintings that were documented during her lifetime either disappeared or were ascribed to others.

So far, about 60 works have been attributed to Artemisia, 40 of which are in public collections. Art historians, however, are increasingly examining 17th-century canvases in the hope of identifying more of her paintings. In just a few years, two versions of *Lucretia*, dating from around 1630, were sold at auction. In 2018, the Viennese auction house Dorotheum sold one for $2.1 million; a year later, the Getty Museum's *Lucretia* appeared. Curators and collectors hope many more works by this talented artist will emerge from the shadows of misattribution.

Lucretia, by Artemisia Gentileschi (c.1627)

Zodiac Fountain Water Clock

Giuseppe Castiglione

1759

The Horse's Head, displayed in 2020

I n 1860, at the height of the Second Opium War, British and French troops swarmed through Beijing's Old Summer Palace (Yuanmingyuan), ransacking the pavilions and then setting them alight. The imperial residence contained jade vases and carvings, porcelain, and gold ornaments. Among the looted treasures were 12 bronze heads, representing the signs of the Chinese zodiac.

The heads – of a snake, horse, goat, monkey, rat, ox, tiger, dragon, pig, dog, cockerel, and rabbit – were part of a water-powered clock made by the 18th-century Italian artist and Jesuit missionary Giuseppe Castiglione. They topped stone figures around a pool in front of the Haiyantang (Hall of the Calm Sea). Every two hours, one of the heads would spout water, as the ancient Chinese day was split into 12 two-hour periods. At noon, they all spouted water.

Reconstruction of the Zodiac Fountain Water Clock, Beijing, 2020

" Before history, one of the two bandits will be called France, the other will be called England. "

Victor Hugo, 1861

In recent years, seven heads have been repatriated to China. In 2000, the Poly Art Museum in Beijing bought the tiger, monkey, and ox heads, which were joined in 2003 by the pig, bought at auction by Hong Kong businessman Stanley Ho. Four years later, Ho bought the horse's head for $8.9 million and gave it to the Capital Museum in Beijing. In 2013, the Pinault family, owners of Christie's auction house, bought the rat and the rabbit, which had been in the art collection of fashion designer Yves St Laurent, and gave them to the National Museum of China.

In 2018, the auction house Tessier et Sarrou in Paris sold a dragon's head for $3.4 million. Speculation was rife that it was one of the missing zodiac heads, but the auction house believed it to come from a later period. Two centuries after the destruction of the palace, the dragon, snake, goat, dog, and cockerel are still missing.

Anna Feodorovna

+——————————•————————————•————————————+

Elisabeth Vigée Le Brun

1796

The 18th-century French artist Elisabeth Vigée Le Brun was celebrated for her portraits of leading figures of the day and enjoyed the patronage of the French queen, Marie-Antoinette. But when the French Revolution began in 1789, she fled the country and spent the next 12 years working in Italy, Russia, and Prussia, where she painted members of various European royal families. Among these works were two portraits of the Grand Duchess Anna Feodorovna of Russia.

While the fate of one portrait is unknown, a second one, painted in 1796, around the time of the duchess's marriage, was thought to have gone missing during World War II. Before the war, it was recorded as being in the Herzogliches Museum in Gotha, northern Germany. In around 1945, it disappeared from there, leading to speculation that it had either been destroyed in bombing raids or looted by Russian soldiers.

In the early 1990s, curators at the Pushkin State Museum of Fine Arts in Moscow were preparing for an exhibition of art lost during World War II when they identified a portrait in a museum storage room as Vigée Le Brun's missing *Anna Feodorovna*. Although they had scarcely any details about the newly discovered painting's provenance, they were able to confirm their hunch by comparing it with a copy that had been made in the mid-19th century. Anna Feodorovna was the aunt of Queen Victoria, and in 1844 the Queen's husband, Prince Albert, had commissioned the English painter William Corden the Younger to make a copy of Vigée Le Brun's portrait. The copy is in the Royal Collection, and the original remains in the collection of the Pushkin Museum.

Anna Feodorovna, painted by Elisabeth Vigée Le Brun in 1796

“ She must have been about
sixteen and the most lively exuberance
shone through her features. ”

Elisabeth Vigée Le Brun

The Death of Cleopatra

———◇———

Edmonia Lewis

1876

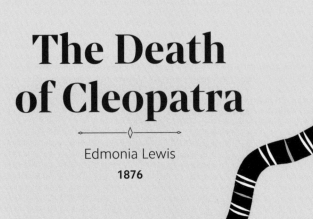

“ Lewis showed the legendary queen of ancient Egypt on her throne. The lifeless body with head tilting back and arms splaying open portrays a vivid realism uncharacteristic of the late 19th century. ”

Alice George, *Smithsonian Magazine*, 2019

Acclaimed for its realism, *The Death of Cleopatra* by Black American sculptor Edmonia Lewis was one of the most-talked-about pieces on display at the Centennial Exposition in Philadelphia in 1876. Yet, despite its popularity, the marble statue remained all but forgotten for the next 100 years.

Lewis had shipped *The Death of Cleopatra* to Philadelphia from Rome, where she lived and worked as a successful sculptor after attending art college in Oberlin, Ohio. The exposition brought her an admiring public, mesmerized by her portrayal of the lifeless figure of Cleopatra reclining on her throne just after the moment of death. When the exposition was over, Lewis could not afford to ship the statue back to Rome, so it stayed in the US. In 1878, it was displayed at the Chicago Interstate Industrial Exposition, but failed to sell. It later spent some time in a Chicago saloon, before being purchased by the owner of the Harlem Race Track in the Forest Park suburb of Chicago. It was installed in front of the grandstand to mark the grave of the man's favourite horse – Cleopatra. The statue remained in place for several decades, despite the ownership of the land changing several times.

In 1982, the statue, by now somewhat damaged, was given to the Forest Park Historical Society. Put into storage, it disappeared from sight. The statue was rediscovered when the art historian Marilyn Richardson began researching her biography of Lewis several years later. In 1988, the statue's true identity was confirmed, based on a photograph from the 1876 exhibition. The Forest Park Historical Society gave the statue to the Smithsonian American Art Museum in Washington, D.C.

The Death of Cleopatra by Edmonia Lewis, 1876

Modern Woman

Mary Cassatt

1893

" People were fascinated
by what women would come
up with as public art. **"**

Wanda Corn, historian

A black-and-white photograph of the centre panel of Cassatt's mural, published in *Harper's Magazine* at the time of the World's Fair

I n 1892, the American painter Mary Cassatt was the first female artist to receive a public art commission in the US when she was asked to paint a vast mural for the Woman's Building at the 1893 Chicago World's Fair. The mural, *Modern Woman*, was for the northern tympanum in the Hall of Honor of the Woman's Building.

Cassatt had studied art at the Pennsylvania Academy of Fine Arts before settling in Paris in 1874. She was associated with the Impressionists, and was on friendly terms with Edgar Degas and Edouard Manet. Painted in France and transported to Chicago, the mural had three panels measuring 17.6 m (58 ft) wide and 3.6 m (12 ft) high in total. The centre panel, titled *Young Women Plucking the Fruits of Knowledge and Science*, was flanked by *Art, Music, Dancing* on the right and *Young Girls Pursuing Fame* on the left. Some viewers were shocked by the women's activities and casual clothing, while others criticized the mural for the absence of any male figures.

When the exhibition closed, all of the exhibits were removed, and the pavilions dismantled. The murals in the Hall of Honor were placed in storage, and subsequently disappeared. It can only be assumed that they were destroyed or that they disintegrated due to neglect.

The Battle of San Jacinto

Henry Arthur McArdle

1901

Attics often offer surprises for art hunters. In 2009, while Jon Buell was rummaging in his grandparents' attic at their home in West Virginia, he uncovered a canvas that had been painted by his great great-grandfather, Henry Arthur McArdle. The canvas was later identified as *The Battle of San Jacinto*, painted in 1901.

McArdle had produced two battle scenes for the Senate chamber of the Texas State Capitol, *The Battle of San Jacinto* (1895), depicting the victorious battle of the Texas Revolution in 1836, and *Dawn at the Alamo* (1905). The 1901 *Battle of San Jacinto* was a smaller version of the original. The family sold the 1901 version in 2010 for $334,000.

Basements also yield up artistic treasures long believed lost. When a family in Essex County, New Jersey, put their parents' house on the market in 2015, they auctioned several items, including a small painting. The canvas turned out to be *Unconscious Patient (Allegory of Smell*; 1624–25), one of five allegorical canvases depicting the five senses painted by Dutch artist Rembrandt van Rijn. Four paintings in the series have now been identified, but the fifth has never been found.

Red and Green II

Georgia O'Keeffe

1916

W hen looking back over their careers, many artists dispose of some of their early work. The American artist Georgia O'Keeffe once asked her New York agent and friend Doris Bry to destroy *Red and Green II* (1916), one of her early watercolours. Bry, however, kept the work, in the hope that O'Keeffe would one day change her mind.

This was not the first time that O'Keefe had her requests ignored. In 1916, while still an art teacher in Texas and before her recognition as a professional artist, O'Keeffe's friend and future husband, Alfred Stieglitz, included some of her work at an exhibition in his gallery in New York. Georgia wrote to Stieglitz, asking him to remove the works as she had not authorized their inclusion, but he refused. As a result, her work found an appreciative audience on the East Coast and her career as a successful artist took off.

When O'Keeffe asked Bry to destroy *Red and Green II*, she made a note of the instruction in her records. The watercolour was more abstract and experimental than the vibrant flower paintings, scenes of New Mexico, and New York skylines that she became famous for. It had been exhibited only once, in New York in 1958, and it was generally thought that only a black-and-white photograph of the work survived.

Following Bry's death in 2014, the Doris Bry Trust offered her collection of works on paper, including work by O'Keeffe, to Christie's auction house in New York. *Red and Green II* was among the 26 works, and sold for $75,000.

Reclining Nude

◇

Amedeo Modigliani

1917

In March 2017, a large poster hung over the entrance to the Palazzo Ducale in the Italian port of Genoa, advertising an exhibition devoted to the career of Amedeo Modigliani. Thousands of visitors filed through the ducal apartments to see the works of one of Italy's most revered modern artists, but three days before the exhibition was due to close, the Italian state fraud squad confiscated 21 of the works.

After analysis, 20 of the 21 works were declared to be forgeries, including a *Reclining Nude* (*Nu couché*) painted in 1917. A number of suspects were charged with forgery and receiving counterfeit works. Modigliani had died in Paris in 1920, almost penniless. Yet within a few years of his death, collectors were paying large sums for his paintings. In 2015, one of his reclining nudes sold at Christie's for $170 million.

Given Modigliani's premature death at 35, without his art being fully documented, curators have struggled to catalogue his work. Forgers saw an opportunity and filled private and public collections with around 1,000 imitations. Art experts claim that only 339 works attributed to Modigliani are indisputably by him. Other genuine works are probably lost among the forgeries.

A genuine *Reclining Nude* (*Nu couché*) by Modigliani sold for $170 million in 2015.

Modigliani is just one of many artists whose reputation is affected by large numbers of forgeries. Experts believe that 50 per cent of all artworks on sale are fakes. One of the most successful forgers, Wolfgang Beltracchi, was exposed in 2008 when *Red Picture with Horses*, supposedly painted by Dutch artist Heinrich Campendonk, was shown to contain titanium white, a pigment that did not exist in 1914, the date Beltracchi claimed the canvas was painted. In 2011, Beltracchi was convicted of forging 14 paintings and sentenced to three years in prison. He went on to make large sums of money painting original works.

> " Modigliani seemed to have painted more pictures after death than when he was alive. "

Carlo Pepi, art critic

December in Venice

Charles Polowetski

1937

In 2008, a visitor to an exhibition at the 19th-century Mills Mansion in Mount Morris, upstate New York, paid $2 to enter, then removed a valuable painting from the wall and left. That, at least, is the working hypothesis of the Hudson Valley police who investigated the scene of the robbery. Unable to find any trace of the thief on security cameras, the museum has given up hope of locating *December in Venice*, painted in 1937 by the Polish-born émigré artist Charles Polowetski. Measuring 76 cm by 60 cm (30 in by 24 in), the painting is a scene, possibly imaginary, of a canal in Venice.

Born in Bielsk in 1884, Polowetski arrived in the US in 1892 and grew up in New York. He went on to train as an artist in Paris, but returned to the US in 1915. Known as a landscape and portrait painter, he was working in New York during the 1930s, where he

> **"** Unfortunately, many of these pieces have been missing for decades ... And (until now) people didn't even know we were looking for them. **"**
>
> **Brian Miller**, former Inspector General for the General Services Administration

received financial support under the Works Progress Administration's Federal Art Project (FAP). Part of a programme of public works to aid recovery from the Great Depression, the FAP employed artists to produce work for public institutions. At the time of the theft, *December in Venice* was on loan to the Mills Mansion from the New Deal Gallery in Mount Morris, which has around 230 FAP paintings by New York artists.

During the 1930s, the FAP commissioned about 200,000 paintings. Many of them are no longer in their original location, and only about 20,000 have been identified. The fate of *December in Venice* is unknown, but as FAP works cannot be bought or sold without the permission of the federal authorities, it has no value. The General Services Administration is in the process of locating surviving FAP paintings. While some were destroyed, it is probable that thousands more lie in attics, basements, or garages, awaiting somebody to recognize them and rescue them from oblivion.

The Reaper

Joan Miró

1937

In 1936, the Catalan artist Joan Miró moved to Paris to escape Spain's brutal civil war (1936–39), which had broken out between the country's Republican government and Nationalist forces led by General Franco. Soon after this, Spain's Republican government commissioned Miró to paint a mural celebrating the country's farm workers for the Spanish Pavilion at the Paris World's Fair of 1937.

Miró painted the mural, titled *The Reaper*, directly onto six insulation panels lining the wall of a stairwell in the pavilion; it measured 5.5 m (18 ft) high and was visible from two floors. As Miró contemplated the poverty of Spanish field workers, and the horrors of the war in his homeland, the work developed a political dimension for him. It featured a peasant in a traditional Catalan red cap, or *barretina*, brandishing a sickle in one hand and holding the other hand in a clenched fist, the Republican salute. Miro's alternative title for the painting was *Catalan Peasant in Revolt*. He said that he included the sickle because it is "the reaper's symbol, the tool of his work, and when his freedom is threatened his weapon", not as a symbol of communism.

When the exhibition was over, Miró gave *The Reaper* to the Republican government in Spain, and it was dismantled and packed into crates for transport. There are various theories about what happened next. Some experts believe it was destroyed en route to Spain, others that it was put into storage somewhere. Another possibility is that the insulation panels on which it was painted disintegrated, though others from this time survived intact. Whatever the cause of its disappearance, *The Reaper* has not been seen since.

Miró working on *The Reaper* at the Paris World Fair, 1937

" Of course I intended it as a protest. "

Joan Miró

47

The Wounded Table

Frida Kahlo

1940

Frida Kahlo working on *The Wounded Table*, 1940

> **❝ As [Kahlo's] profile has risen, theories regarding her oeuvre have proliferated, making it difficult to distinguish fact from fiction. ❞**
>
> *Smithsonian Magazine*, 2020

A year after Mexican artist Frida Kahlo's death in 1954, her vast painting *The Wounded Table* (*La Mesa Herida*) disappeared while on loan to a gallery in Warsaw. It has never been seen since.

Kahlo worked on the painting during the winter of 1939–40, following her divorce from her husband, the painter Diego Rivera. Measuring 1.22 m by 2.44 m (approximately 4 ft by 8 ft), the huge canvas gave her an opportunity to explore the sense of betrayal, death, and despair that she felt at the breakdown of her marriage. Kahlo sits behind a wooden table that has human legs and feet. She is flanked by a skeleton, a piece of native Mexican art, her pet deer, and her niece and nephew. Kahlo worked rapidly as she had agreed to show the painting at the International Exhibition of Surrealism in Mexico City, which opened in February 1940.

After the exhibition, Kahlo hung *The Wounded Table* in her house for a number of years, before giving it to the Russian ambassador as a gift to the Soviet Union. The painting was sent to Moscow and put into storage. In 1955, it was loaned to the Zachęta National Gallery of Art in Warsaw. Once the exhibition was over, the painting disappeared.

No one has been able to discover the fate of The *Wounded Table*, although a number of art dealers have purported to possess the original. A claim by Spanish dealer Cristian López Márquez in 2020 was dismissed. Fans of Kahlo's work hope that it may yet turn up in a museum storeroom. Meanwhile, a replica based on photographs of the original painting, including one with the artist seated beside it, is on display at the Frida Kahlo Museum in the German city of Baden-Baden.

Struggle: From the History of the American People

Jacob Lawrence

1954–56

Exhibitions can be a good way to find lost masterpieces. Between 1954 and 1956, the American artist Jacob Lawrence produced a series of 30 paintings depicting the struggle of his fellow Black Americans to obtain basic civil rights. Lawrence originally intended to paint 60 panels, covering the period from European colonization to World War I, but funding ran out, and in 1959, he was obliged to sell the 30 he had completed – covering 1775 to 1817. A private collector purchased the set and later sold the paintings individually. Over time, people lost track of the whereabouts of several panels, and they were considered lost.

Some 60 years later, in 2020, the Metropolitan Museum of Art in New York staged *The American Struggle*, an exhibition of the 25 known panels. A visitor to the exhibition realized that he had seen a painting on his friends' wall that closely resembled the work on display. Could it be one of the missing panels? The painting was owned by an elderly New York couple, who had purchased it at a charity sale in about 1960. It was authenticated as Panel 16, and the couple, who wished to remain anonymous, offered it to the exhibition.

Good fortune soon struck again. When a nurse read about the discovery, she examined a painting on her apartment wall. It had been a gift from her mother-in-law, who had stuck a newspaper article

Panel 16 of Jacob Lawrence's *Struggle: From the History of the American People*

" *American Struggle* at the Met shows an artist searching out bits of the nation's history that have been edged out. "

The New York Times, 2020

about Lawrence to the back of the work. To her surprise, she found that the canvas was signed by Jacob Lawrence. When her son looked up the Metropolitan Museum's online catalogue, he saw that the work was listed as Panel 28 "Immigrants admitted from all countries: 1820 to 1840 – 115,773."– location unknown. The nurse contacted the museum, which dispatched curators to authenticate the Lawrence hanging on her wall. Now there are just three panels missing, numbers 14, 20, and 29.

Life's Work

Vivian Maier

1950s–1990s

" I don't think she liked kids
at all really. I think she liked
images. When she saw an
image she had to capture it. "

Joe Matthews, former charge of Vivian Maier, 2014

Little escaped the eye of street photographer Vivian Maier, but her talent was not recognized until after her death, when the remnants of her collection were rescued from destruction. It is impossible to guess how many prints and negatives were destroyed, or were never developed.

Although there is no definitive archive, it is estimated that Maier took more than 100,000 photographs over five decades. What makes her photographs of Chicago, New York, and Los Angeles unique is her viewpoint. She saw everything as valuable and worthy of recording for posterity, from scenes of industrial decay to children playing, workers window-shopping during their lunch break, and down-and-outs eking out a living.

Born in New York, Maier worked as a nanny and then as a housekeeper in Chicago. In her mid-20s, she developed a passion for photography and spent her spare time wandering the streets, taking snapshots of strangers with her Rolleiflex camera. In 1956, she began developing and printing her own work, possibly in order to save money. In 1959, she took a trip around the world, visiting the Philippines, Thailand, China, India, Syria, Egypt, and Italy. Everywhere she went, she took candid photographs. When colour photography developed, she switched to that.

Maier rarely showed her photographs to anybody, and for a long time she kept her work in boxes at her employers' houses. As her collection – which also included newspaper cuttings and interviews with some of her subjects – expanded, she rented storage space in Chicago. By 2007, she could no longer keep up payments and the storage company auctioned her photographs and negatives. Three photo collectors purchased the work and began uploading it to the internet. Other collectors began to take note of her eclectic archive.

By this stage, Maier was living in poverty and no longer pursued her interest in photography. After slipping on ice and hitting her head in 2008, her health deteriorated, and she died the following year. But she was to enjoy posthumous fame. The number of collectors of her work increased, and three documentaries have been made about the extraordinary lives and times captured by the nanny from New York.

Untitled Gouache

◦———◇———◦

Jackson Pollock

1940s

Most people in the art world can only dream of finding a lost work of art, but Josh Levine, an appraiser and auctioneer in Scottsdale, Arizona, has lived that dream. In 2015, an elderly man who was moving into a retirement home called him to clear out a garage in Sun City. When Levine came across an unsigned gouache he suspected was the work of Jackson Pollock, a leading proponent of American Abstract Expressionism, he thought his dreams had come true.

Levine employed a forensic expert and investigative team to analyse the work. They found that the pigments used were typical of mid-20th century paints, and the brushwork was similar to that in other work produced by Pollock. However, this was not absolute proof that the work was by the artist. For two years, the auctioneer tried to trace where the painting had come from. He learned that it had been bequeathed to the owner of the garage by his half-sister, socialite Jenifer Cosgriff, who had moved in Pollock's New York circle.

The auctioneer is convinced the work is genuine, but unless the work is authenticated, he cannot sell it. If it is a genuine Jackson Pollock, it may be worth up to $15 million. Had Levine not spotted the work and identified it, the gouache may well have ended up in a charity shop.

The Lenin Mosaic

Vladimir Tverdokhlebov

1984

I n 2018, a vast mosaic portrait of Vladimir Lenin, a founder and former president of the Soviet Union, was one of a number of monumental works of art uncovered in the city of Almaty, the former capital of Kazakhstan. Created in 1984 by Vladimir Tverdokhlebov, a member of Kazakhstan's monumental art movement, the mosaic, measuring 4 m by 5 m (13 ft by 16.5 ft), had been boarded up in the city's Academy of Science. Although now saved, the image of Lenin is kept covered by a curtain due to political sensitivity.

During the Soviet era, monumental public art adorned buildings in cities and towns all over the USSR. Central Asia was no exception. Local artists produced huge, colourful mosaics and murals celebrating daily life, military, sporting, and technological achievements, and political subjects. Dozens of such works were installed around Almaty between the 1960s and the end of the 1980s.

Not all member states had wanted to be part of the Soviet Union, and monumental art became hostage to changing political fortunes. With the collapse of communism, many of the artworks were neglected, boarded up, or painted over. In some former member states, such as Ukraine, Soviet art was banned altogether. The survival of Almaty's art is probably due to the fact that the city ceased to be the capital of Kazakhstan in 1997. New construction in the city declined, so old buildings containing such art were less likely to be demolished.

The value of this public art in the cities of Central Asia is gradually being realized. Because it reflected local traditions and folklore, as well as serving Soviet values, local volunteers are working to uncover and preserve what is left of it.

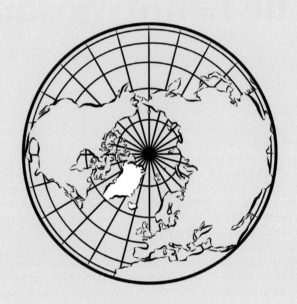

Touching
North

Andy Goldswothy

1989

" The North Pole belongs to no one – it is the Earth's common – an everchanging landscape in which whatever I make will disappear. "

Andy Goldsworthy, 1989

In April 1989, the British artist Andy Goldsworthy constructed a set of four large, upright circles from blocks of ice. Known as *Touching North*, the four circles were positioned around the North Pole. The artist had learned the technique of cutting and stacking blocks of ice from an Inuit person living in northern Canada. Before he left the North Pole, Goldsworthy photographed the sculpture, knowing that the ice would eventually melt.

Long fascinated by the transience of art, Goldsworthy is a leading exponent of site-specific and land art. He works only with materials that he finds in nature, such as wood, stone, leaves, mud, petals, and sand, which he arranges, shapes, carves, or builds to create ephemeral works in the landscape that he expects will change after he has finished them. He also uses water in all its forms – vapour, liquid, and ice. He often photographs his work over a period of time after it is finished to record how the artwork "grows, stays, and decays."

Artists have long used unusual materials to carve ephemeral works, sometimes for novelty value rather than to convey a concept. In the 16th century, aristocratic courts commissioned carvings in butter, sugar, and ice as table decorations. An apocryphal tale recounts how the 18th-century Italian sculptor, Antonio Canova, came to the attention of a wealthy art patron when, as a child, he carved a lion from a block of butter. Modern artists other than Goldsworthy who work in ephemeral media include Brazilian artist Néle Azevedo, who, in 2009, carved 1,000 sitting figures from ice in order to draw attention to climate change. The work, *Melting Men*, was installed on a staircase in a square in Berlin.

Stolen

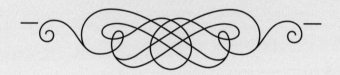

Mexican Antiquities

7th century CE

When security guards at the National Museum of Anthropology in Mexico City switched on the lights early on Christmas morning in 1985, they could not believe their eyes. Seven glass cases lay open and much of the museum's collection from the Mayan sites of Palenque and Chichén Itzá were missing. All of the stolen items dated from pre-Columbian times and included the jade death mask of the seventh-century ruler Pakal the Great and an obsidian monkey-vase.

The thieves had chosen a good night to strike, as Christmas Eve in Mexico is an important public holiday. The police concluded that the guards had been remiss in their duties after finding alcohol and the remains of a festive dinner. There was no closed-circuit security system with images of the theft, and after two years of fruitless investigation, it seemed likely that the items had gone forever. The authorities did not give up, however, and in 1989 police caught one of the thieves after receiving a tip-off from a drug-trafficker who claimed that two men had tried to sell him an ancient artefact.

It materialized that the theft had been committed by veterinary students Carlos Perches Treviño and Ramón Sardina García. The pair had spent six months visiting the museum, examining possible entry routes. On the night of the theft, they jumped the perimeter fence and entered the Mayan Hall through a broken air-conditioning duct, stealing small objects that were easy to carry. The pair then stored their booty, valued at many millions of US dollars, in a cupboard at Treviño's house and left for Acapulco.

After receiving the tip-off, police arrested Treviño at his home, where most of the loot was still stored. However, to this day Ramón Sardina García is still on the run, but even he may not know where the remaining works are now hidden.

The Book of Kells

c. 800 CE

A set of the Gospels of Matthew, Mark, Luke, and John, *The Book of Kells* is one of the oldest illuminated manuscripts in existence. The book's origins are lost in the mists of time, but it is thought to have been completed around 800 CE by monks at the monastery founded by St Colomba on the Scottish island of Iona. In 806, some 68 monks at the monastery were massacred in a Viking raid, and the survivors moved to a Colomban monastery at Kells in County Meath, Ireland, taking the precious Gospels with them.

In 1006, the book was stolen from the abbey church at Kells. Following a search by all members of the community, it was found buried in a nearby ditch "beneath a sod" several weeks later, according to the 15th-century Annals of Ulster. The wooden cover, inlaid with gold, silver, and gems, was missing and has never been found.

The manuscript represents the pinnacle of Celtic art. The monks wrote on vellum (animal skin), using compasses and rulers to draw designs of extraordinary complexity, which they illuminated with bright colours derived from plants and minerals. Today, 340 leaves from the original manuscript survive, kept at Trinity College Library in Dublin.

The Ghent Altarpiece

Jan and Hubert van Eyck

1432

The celebrated *Adoration of the Mystic Lamb*, also known as the Ghent Altarpiece, in St Bavo's Cathedral, in Ghent, Belgium, has had a tempestuous history since it was painted in the early 15th century by the brothers Jan and Hubert van Eyck. In the mid-15th century it was threatened with destruction by Protestant iconoclasts. Three and a half centuries later, Napoleon had it installed in the Louvre in Paris. During World War II, Nazi soldiers hid it in an Austrian salt mine, from where it was rescued by Allied commandos.

The 12-panel altarpiece did not survive these vicissitudes intact. In April 1934, one of its panels, titled *The Just Judges*, was removed during the night. Two weeks later, the Bishop of Bruges received an anonymous ransom note demanding payment of 1 million Belgian francs for its return. Over the summer, the Belgian government, which took over the negotiations, exchanged a series of notes with the thief, who returned a monochrome painting of St John that formed the back of the panel, as a show of good faith.

In November 1934, a Belgian stockbroker, Arsène Goedertier, confessed to his lawyer on his deathbed that he knew the location of the painting, though he did not reveal it. After his death, carbon copies of the ransom letters were discovered in his desk. But the panel has never been found, and in 1945 a replica of *The Just Judges*, based on a 16th-century copy made for King Philip II of Spain, was installed in the altarpiece.

A section of the Ghent Altarpiece showing a replica of *The Just Judges* (left panel) and *The Knights of Christ* (right panel)

" *The Just Judges* are in a place where neither I nor anyone else can take it without attracting the public's attention. "

Ransom note, 1934

The Last Judgement

Hans Memling

1467–71

In 1473, a privateer named Paul Beneke stole Hans Memling's vast altarpiece *The Last Judgement* from a ship in the English Channel. During the ensuing centuries, this much-admired and sought-after painting crisscrossed Europe several times.

The work was commissioned in 1466 by Angelo Tani, the manager of the Medici bank in Bruges. When completed, it was loaded onto a ship bound for Florence, where Tani intended to place it in his family chapel at Fiesole. Beneke found the painting below deck and transported it to his native Danzig (modern Gdańsk in Poland), where it was installed in the church of St Mary. The work, which presents a vision of the Christian Last Judgment, when the dead are judged by God and sent to either heaven or hell, attracted enormous crowds.

In the 16th century, the Holy Roman Emperor tried in vain to buy the work for his own private chapel, and in 1716, Peter the Great of Russia failed to obtain it as war restitution. In 1807, Napoleon's troops took the altarpiece to the Louvre in Paris, but after Napoleon's defeat, it was sent to Berlin. Two years later, it was returned to St Mary's in Danzig.

Towards the end of World War II, the German army hid the painting in a church in Thuringia, where the Soviet Union's Red Army found it and took it to the Hermitage Museum in Leningrad (today's St Petersburg). It stayed there until 1956, when it was returned to Poland.

> " A human sensibility that blesses each soul, whether saved or damned, with individual personality. "

Rachel Spence, *The Financial Times*, 2014

Hans Memling's, *The Last Judgement*

Mona Lisa

Leonardo da Vinci

1503

Leonardo da Vinci's *Mona Lisa*, 1503

As a plumber passed a doorway in the Louvre Museum in Paris on the morning of Monday 21 August 1911, he saw a man fumbling with a door and opened it for him. The man, a 30-year-old Italian, Vincenzo Peruggia, thanked the plumber and hastily left, carrying Leonardo da Vinci's *Mona Lisa*, wrapped in a work smock, under his arm.

Peruggia, a museum employee, knew the gallery was closed to the public on Mondays and had removed the canvas from its frame in the Salon Carré unnoticed. The empty frame did not immediately attract attention as items were often removed for repair, to be photographed in daylight, or to be sent to other museums on loan. But when a curator enquired where the painting had gone, nobody could explain and the alarm was raised.

Peruggia hid the painting in his lodgings for two years while the police searched for it in vain. Then, in December 1913, he thought he had a buyer. He travelled to Florence to meet an art dealer, who brought the director of the Uffizi gallery to the meeting as well. Peruggia produced the *Mona Lisa* from the false base of his trunk, and the experts agreed to purchase it. But instead, they immediately alerted the police. Peruggia was arrested the following day. Found guilty of theft, he was given a one-year prison sentence, but served only a few months. The *Mona Lisa* returned to Paris after a tour of Italy.

Peruggia claimed that his motive for the theft had been patriotic. He believed – wrongly – that Napoleon had stolen the *Mona Lisa* during the French occupation of northern Italy 100 years earlier. Peruggia said that he had only wanted to return it to its native land.

" [People] didn't come to look at the *Mona Lisa*, they came in order to have seen it. "

Robert Hughes, art critic

St Christopher Carrying the Christ Child

Jan van Eyck

15th century

Jan van Eyck's *St Christopher Carrying the Christ Child*

Some paintings that were well known during an artist's lifetime have gone missing over time, and no one knows why. This happened with the 15th-century Netherlandish artist Jan van Eyck's painting *St Christopher Carrying the Christ Child*.

Van Eyck is known to have painted the story about St Christopher carrying a child on his back across a swollen river. According to legend, when St Christopher reached the far side of the river, he realized he had been carrying the infant Jesus. The story had appeared in a collection of the lives of the saints, the *Golden Legend*, written around 1260 by the Italian chronicler and archbishop Jacobus de Voraigne. This was one of the most popular religious books of the Middle Ages, and it inspired many artists in their choice of subjects. Van Eyck is thought to have painted his version late in his career.

Van Eyck's technical inventiveness and jewel-like colours, due to his innovative use of oil paints and glazes, meant that he was widely admired and copied by his peers. In this case, several celebrated artists, including the Netherlandish Dieric Bouts and the German-born Hans Memling, made copies. However, art scholars are certain that the most accurate copy of Van Eyck's painting was made by an unknown follower of his in around 1460–70, some 20 to 30 years after his death, as it closely resembles a drawing made by a contemporary of Van Eyck. The drawing is now preserved in the Louvre Museum in Paris. The copy, painted in oils on an oak panel, and measuring about 30 cm by 21 cm (11 ¾ in by 8 in), is on display at the Philadelphia Museum of Art.

❝ [Jan van Eyck] set himself to make trial of various sorts of colours and to prepare many kinds of oil for making varnishes and other things dear to men of inventive brain. **❞**

Giorgio Vasari, 1550

The Benin Bronzes

16th century

" Part of the crime is ... that
you've portrayed our civilization
as a dead civilization. **"**

Osarobo Zeickner-Okoro, Nigerian artist
and bronze caster, Benin City, 2021

One of the Benin Bronzes held by the British Museum

In early 1897, British soldiers attacked the royal palace in Benin City, capital of the West African Kingdom of Benin in modern-day Nigeria, and looted hundreds of treasures. The stolen objects included metal plaques known as the Benin Bronzes, which record the history of Benin, as well as human and animal figures, and royal regalia. Items made from other materials, such as ivory, coral, leather, and wood, were also taken. The plunder of the royal treasures, some of which date from the 16th century, has never been forgotten in Nigeria. Successive rulers and governments have demanded their return.

As British traders made inroads along the coast of West Africa in the late 19th century, the British government came up with a proposal to incorporate the Kingdom of Benin into the British Empire. The Oba, or king, of the Edo people of Benin, however, had no interest in his country joining the British Empire, so a contingent of British

British soldiers with objects looted from Benin's Royal Palace, 1897

❝ I would add that I have reason to hope that sufficient ivory would be found in the King's house to pay the expenses incurred in removing the King from his stool. ❞

British Acting Consul Captain James R. Philip, 1896

troops was dispatched to attack Benin City and depose the king, who was captured and sent into exile. Soldiers plundered the royal palace and other sites, and divided the looted treasures among themselves. Then the British Admiralty intervened to confiscate the artefacts in order to defray the cost of the expedition. An estimated 3,000–5,000 objects were shipped back to London, where they were bought by museums and private collectors across Europe. The British Museum received more than 900 items, including the Benin Bronzes. Later that year, the museum put its collection on display.

The Bronzes are of great cultural and religious significance for the people of Nigeria. They are part of the royal effects and they indicate that the Oba rules by divine right and receives his mandate not from the nation, but from the deities that local people have traditionally venerated. Nigeria is determined to get back as many items as possible from international museums that are willing to share or return stolen artefacts.

The returned bronzes will be housed in Nigeria's new Edo Museum of West African Art, next to the royal palace in Benin City. Across Africa, new museums are opening to display the continent's cultural treasures and heritage. The Museum of Black Civilizations in Senegal (opened 2018) and the Palais de Lomé in Togo (opened 2019) set the trend, and are to be followed by the Grand Egyptian Museum in Egypt, the Pan African Heritage World Museum in Ghana, the Museum of Humankind in Kenya, and the Museum of Maritime History in Mozambique.

Returning looted artworks

For more than a century, a bronze cockerel perched on a ledge in the dining hall of Jesus College, Cambridge, in England. Few of the students and staff could have guessed that the bird – known as an *okukor* – had been looted by a British trader, George Neville, who stole 129 bronzes from Benin in 1897. In 2022, the college returned the cockerel to Nigeria and began a review of its historical connections with slave traders who had made donations to the college.

Nativity with
St Francis and
St Lawrence

Caravaggio

1609

O n the night of 17 October 1969, at least two people broke into
the 16th-century Franciscan Oratory of San Lorenzo in the
Sicilian capital of Palermo. They cut a large canvas painted by Italian
artist Caravaggio from its frame above the high altar, wrapped it
in a carpet, and spirited it away. *The Nativity with St Francis and
St Lawrence* has not been seen since. The art world was shocked
when the empty frame was discovered, prompting a discussion
about how a nation can care for its immense artistic heritage.

The *Nativity* had featured on Italian television some weeks
before the theft, perhaps inspiring the thieves to attempt the
audacious robbery on the poorly guarded chapel. The theft quickly
became the subject of speculation and rumour. Police suspected it
had been stolen on the orders of a Mafia crime boss in Sicily.

In the decades since the theft, a number of Mafia informants
claimed to know either the whereabouts or the fate of the
painting. Some sources claimed it had been so badly damaged
during its removal that the thieves were forced to dispose of it;
others that the canvas had been cut up and fed to pigs in order
to leave no trace. None of the various stories have led to the
painting's discovery, and it remains one of the FBI's top ten
international art thefts.

Caravaggio's *Nativity with St Francis and St Lawrence*

“ To steal that painting,
which is three by two metres,
between all of Serpotta's stucco,
you had to plan it and study. ”

Bernardo Tortorici di Raffadali, Friends of Sicilian Museums, 2018

The Head of a Bearded Man

Peter Paul Rubens

1615

R ussborough House near Dublin has proved a honeypot for thieves. The Palladian-style mansion contained the art collection of Sir Alfred Beit, and was robbed four times between 1974 and 2002, resulting in the loss of work by Johannes Vermeer, Peter Paul Rubens, Francisco Goya, Thomas Gainsborough, and many others. Although most works were recovered quickly after each theft, *The Head of a Bearded Man* (1615) painted by Rubens remained lost for 16 years.

The first robbery took place in 1974, when a gang connected to the Irish Republican Army (IRA), which sought to end British rule in Northern Ireland, stole 19 paintings valued at £8 million. Eight days later, Irish police raided a cottage in County Cork and retrieved all the paintings undamaged. Twelve years later, in 1986, a Dublin-based criminal gang led by Martin Cahil took 18 paintings, valued at £30–50 million, including Rubens' *The Head of a Bearded Man*. Several were found within days close to the house, and others surfaced around Europe in the following years. The Rubens portrait was recovered in Dublin in 2002. Two Venetian scenes by Francesco Guardi are thought to be buried somewhere in the Dublin mountains; their exact whereabouts may never be known, as Cahill died in 1994.

Although Russborough House was raided again in 2001 and in 2002, the stolen works were tracked down and returned to the collection. Today, the recovered paintings can be seen in the National Gallery of Ireland in Dublin.

The Head of a Bearded Man by Rubens

" There is a madness that afflicts these people. They are not necessarily art lovers, but they view the works as trophies. "

Charles Hill, international art detective, 2003

Adam and Eve

Georg Petel

1627

George Petel's *Adam and Eve*, 1627

" It's the most beautiful object I have ever seen. "

Stéphane Breitwieser, art thief, 2019

The compulsive art thief Stéphane Breitwieser may hold the world record for high-value kleptomania. The Frenchman has stolen art worth in excess of €1 billion from more than 200 collections across Europe. He claims not to do it for the money, but from an uncontrollable compulsion to steal works of art.

In an interview with *GQ* magazine in 2019, Breitwieser explained that it took him just 10 minutes to unscrew the glass dome protecting an ivory carving of Adam and Eve in the Rubens House Museum in Antwerp. The Dutch sculptor Georg Petel had carved it in 1627, as a 50th birthday present for his friend, the painter Peter Paul Rubens. The 25-cm- (10-in-) high statue shows Adam and Eve standing beside a tree around which a serpent is coiled. That theft took place in 1997, when the fitfully employed young Breitwieser was at his most active.

In November 2001, Breitwieser was arrested after stealing a bugle from the Richard Wagner Museum in Switzerland. It is thought that his girlfriend and accomplice, Anne-Catherine Kleinklaus, fled back to France to alert Breitwieser's mother, Mireille Stengel. Together, the two women loaded a car with hundreds of objects from Breitwieser's house and threw them into a nearby canal. A few days later, a passing walker noticed something glinting in the water and alerted the police. It turned out to be a gold-plated chalice.

When police dredged the canal, they found objects worth hundreds of thousands of euros, including the Adam and Eve ivory by Petel. The piece was carefully restored and returned to the Rubens House Museum.

The Isabella Stewart Gardner Heist

Vermeer's *The Concert* and works by other artists

1664

Johannes Vermeer's *The Concert*

In the early hours of 18 March 1990, two thieves broke into Boston's Isabella Stewart Gardner Museum and pulled off one of the most daring heists in modern American history. In just 81 minutes, they removed 13 of the priceless paintings and drawings from the collection amassed by philanthropist and collector Isabella Stewart Gardner.

The thieves, dressed in stolen police uniforms, arrived at a museum side door and told the two security guards on duty that they were responding to an alert. After gaining entrance, the thieves quickly overpowered the guards, bound them with duct tape, and locked them in the museum basement, before disabling the surveillance cameras. They then moved rapidly through the darkened building, removing paintings from walls and nimbly extracting, and in some cases cutting, the canvases from their frames. They carried out two trips to a car, and then made their getaway at 2.45 am. As they left, they removed a cassette tape that had recorded the robbery.

" Something that might inspire people – that might transform lives is missing. "

Alan Chong, curator, Isabella Stewart Gardner Museum, 2010

Anxious to escape quickly, the robbers had targeted smaller works. They took three by Rembrandt van Rijn – *Christ in the Storm on the Sea of Galilee* (1663), his only seascape, *A Lady and Gentleman in Black* (1633), and a small self-portrait from the Dutch Room, together with *Landscape with Obelisk* (1638) by Rembrandt's pupil, Govaert Flinck, and a Chinese bronze *gu*, or beaker, dating from the 12th century BCE. Five sketches by Edgar Degas disappeared from another ground-floor room, together with a Napoleonic brass flag finial in the form of an eagle. The thieves took Edouard Manet's painting *Chez Tortoni* (also known as *Man in a Silk Hat*) (*c.*1875) from a first-floor room. The most valuable painting to be stolen, however, also from

SEEKING INFORMATION

BY THE FBI

The FBI is seeking information in the theft of thirteen works of art from the Isabella Stewart Gardner Museum in 1990.

The Storm on the Sea of Galilee
REMBRANDT, 1633
Oil on canvas, 161.7 x 129.8 cm
Inscribed on the rudder: Rembrandt (sic). f::/ 1633

$5 Million Reward

The FBI encourages anyone who may have information on the whereabouts of the artwork to contact the FBI at 1-800-CALL-FBI or submit online at Tips.FBI.Gov.

An FBI poster offers a $5 million reward for information in 2013

" Were the works taken for love, money, ransom, glory, barter or for some tangled combination of them all? "

Robert M. Poole, *Smithsonian Magazine*, 2005

the Dutch Room, was *The Concert* by Johannes Vermeer. It depicts an intimate domestic scene in which a young woman sings, accompanied perhaps by her music teacher on the lute and another pupil at the harpsichord. It is one of only 34 paintings attributed to Vermeer in the world, and is valued by the museum at $250 million.

The next morning, staff arrived to find the guards still tied up in the basement. After the Boston Police Department made a preliminary inspection, the FBI took charge of the investigation. At the time, the stolen works were valued at more than $200 million, and a reward of $1 million was offered for information leading to their recovery.

The identity of the thieves has never been definitively established. In 2015, the FBI confirmed that its two main suspects had both died. It indicated that they were members of the Boston Mafia, and possibly had accomplices, but no one has ever been charged. As the statute of limitations (the deadline by which legal proceedings can be brought) passed in 1995, no prosecutions can now be made. Given their fame, the works could never be sold on the open market.

The current offer by the museum of a $10 million reward leading to the recovery of all the works remains unclaimed. Isabella Stewart Gardner left her collection in trust with an endowment that allows it to be opened to the public, but with the proviso that all the works remain as she had arranged them. If the display changes, the collection must be shipped to Paris and sold at auction. To keep to the terms of the will and in mute tribute to the missing works, the empty frames left behind by the thieves still hang in their original positions on the walls.

Isabella Stewart Gardner

Born in 1840, the daughter of a wealthy New York linen merchant, Isabella Stewart married John Gardner in 1860 and moved to Boston. After their only child died just short of his second birthday, the couple began travelling widely. On visits to Europe, Russia, Scandinavia, and Asia, they indulged their passion for buying art, which they shipped back to their home in Boston. Following her husband's sudden death in 1898, Isabella commissioned a building in her favourite style – that of a Renaissance Venetian palace – to house the collection, so that it could be opened to the public.

Lioness and Lion in a Cave

Eugène Delacroix

1856

Public holidays are good days to break into a museum, as three criminals had predicted when they broke into the Montreal Museum of Fine Arts on Labor Day, 4 September 1972. They pulled off the biggest art theft in Canadian history – one that remains unsolved.

At about midnight, the thieves climbed onto the museum roof and descended through an unsecured skylight on a rope. Threatening the security guards with a gun, they tied them up, and proceeded to help themselves to the artworks before fleeing through a side exit. The guards were unable to provide much information as the intruders wore ski masks, but they noted that two spoke French and one English. The men escaped with 18 paintings, including Eugène Delacroix's *Lioness and Lion in a Cave* (1856). They had also filled their pockets with jewellery. The value of the stolen items was estimated at $2 million.

A few days after the theft, an anonymous caller instructed a member of staff go to a nearby phone booth. Answering the phone there, the museum director was told to pick up a cigarette packet that had been left nearby. Inside was a pendant from the haul, which was meant to indicate that the thieves might strike a deal. For several

Eugène Delacroix's *Lioness and Lion in a Cave*, 1856

❝ Tigers, panthers, jaguars, lions, etc.
Why is it that these things
have stirred me so much? ❞

Eugène Delacroix, 1847

weeks, phone calls and letters passed to and fro, until the thieves demanded $500,000 for the return of the items, before agreeing to half the sum. To prove that they still had the art, the thieves returned one of two paintings by Bruegel the Elder.

The cat-and-mouse game continued into the summer, but eventually proved fruitless. For more than half a century, works by Bruegel the Elder, Delacroix, Peter Paul Rubens, Jean-Baptiste-Camille Corot, Gustave Courbet, Honoré Daumier, and Thomas Gainsborough have remained missing.

Les Choristes

Edgar Degas

1877

" The recovery of *Les Choristes* is really just the starting gun for the unravelling of the mystery of its theft. "

Guy Martin, *Forbes Magazine*, 2018

Edgar Degas' *Les Choristes*, 1877

W hen French customs officers stopped a bus near Paris in February 2017, they were surprised to find a drawing by the French Impressionist Edgar Degas in the luggage compartment. The officers who operated the checkpoint at Ferrières-en-Brie were making a random check for illegal drugs. They became suspicious when none of the passengers claimed one of the cases. On opening the case, they discovered a carefully wrapped pastel drawing of a line of male singers in late 19th-century dress. In the lower left corner was the giveaway signature – Degas.

With no claimants among the passengers, police confiscated the case. A few days later, the drawing was confirmed as *Les Choristes* (*The Chorus Singers*). It had been stolen nine years earlier from the Musée Cantini in Marseilles while on loan from the Musée d'Orsay in Paris.

Closed-circuit surveillance cameras failed to yield any images of people loading luggage onto the bus, and none of the passengers could provide information. The police and museum authorities had to be content that the stolen drawing, valued at €800,000, had been found.

Funerary Pole

19th century

In June 2020, a group of five visitors walked into the Quai Branly Museum in Paris. After looking at some of the displays, one of the men began to berate France for stealing Africa's cultural artefacts. As a companion filmed him on a mobile phone, the man turned to a 19th-century wooden funerary pole from the Chad and Sudan region of central Africa and removed it from its bracket. Stopped by security guards as he tried to leave the museum, he said that the French had stolen the artefact, and that he intended to free it. In September 2020, Emery Mwazulu Diyabanza and his companions, who call themselves Les Marrons Unis Dignes et Courageux (The United Worthy and Courageous Maroons), were tried for attempted theft and collectively fined €2,000.

Diyabanza, a restitution activist who was born in the Democratic Republic of the Congo, received all the publicity he wanted when his companion live-streamed the attempted theft on social media. The museum contains some 70,000 objects from non-European countries. A 2018 report commissioned by the French authorities concluded that 90 to 95 per cent of sub-Saharan cultural artefacts are in the hands of museums or private collectors outside Africa. France holds approximately 90,000 objects. The report also stated that such items should be returned if requested, but very few have been.

Despite arrests and fines, Diyabanza and his companions continue to take objects from museums across Europe, broadcasting their actions on the internet in order to raise public awareness and debate about the true ownership of looted works.

Activist Emery Mwazulu Diyabanza in Paris, 2020

" We shouldn't need to ask thieves for permission to take back what they stole. "

Emery Mwazulu Diyabanza, 2020

Summer's Day

◆

Berthe Morisot

1879

On 14 April 1956, two young Irishmen took Berthe Morisot's *Summer's Day* (1879) from the wall of the Tate Gallery in London and absconded with it. Art student Paul Hogan and his friend, veterinary student William Fogerty, claimed that the theft was part of a campaign to have the painting returned to Ireland.

The robbery was the essence of simplicity. Hogan often visited the Tate Gallery to draw, and was on nodding terms with several members of staff. When the room was empty, he removed the painting from the wall and slipped it into his portfolio. As Hogan left the gallery, he was snapped by a press photographer who had been tipped off in advance, in order to gain publicity for the stunt. Four days later, a friend of the pair left the painting at the Irish Embassy in London, and it was returned to the gallery undamaged.

The students claimed that they wanted to highlight a long-standing dispute over the will of Hugh Lane, founder of Dublin's Municipal Gallery of Modern Art (now the Hugh Lane Gallery), who had died in May 1915. Under the terms of the will, written in 1913, Lane bequeathed his collection of 39 paintings to London, where they were already on display. But after his death an unwitnessed codicil dated February 1915 was found that left his paintings to the City of Dublin, suggesting he had changed his mind. Nonetheless, the paintings went to London.

The students argued that as Lane had died unexpectedly in the sinking of the RMS *Lusitania* in May 1915 while returning from a trip to the US, he had not had the opportunity to rewrite his will. They were taking up the cause of Lane's aunt, Lady Augusta Gregory, who had spent many years before her death in 1932 trying to convince the British government that her nephew's

" We were enormously successful in putting the issue in the headlines. "

Paul Hogan, 2015

intention to donate his collection to Ireland was clear. Many famous writers had supported Lady Gregory's cause, including William Butler Yeats and George Bernard Shaw.

Three years after the theft, in 1959, the Irish and British authorities agreed to share the paintings. In 1993, the agreement was changed to allow 27 paintings to remain in Ireland and four in London. The remaining pictures were divided into two groups, which would alternate each year between London and Dublin.

Summer's Day by Berthe Morisot, 1879

View of the Sea
at Scheveningen

Vincent van Gogh

1882

O n 7 December 2002, thieves used a sledgehammer to smash a window at the Van Gogh Museum in Amsterdam and stole *View of the Sea at Scheveningen* and *Congregation Leaving the Reformed Church in Nuenen*. Fourteen years later, the two paintings were found in the home of an Italian drug-dealer.

The trail leading to the recovery of the paintings began with the arrest of Octave Durham in Marbella, Spain, in 2003. Durham was implicated in the crime through DNA evidence gathered from strands of hair in a baseball cap that had been lost in the heist. He served a 25-month prison sentence, but refused to cooperate with police investigations into the whereabouts of the paintings.

In fact, Durham and his accomplice, Henk Bieslijn, had sold the paintings to an Italian drug-dealer named Raffaele Imperiale. In August 2016, Imperiale wrote to a public prosecutor in Naples to say that he had bought the two paintings, possibly with the intention of using them as bargaining chips against narcotics charges. The following month, Italian police raided Imperiale's family farmhouse near Naples, where they found the paintings in a wall cavity, wrapped in cotton sheets.

In a documentary about the heist, Durham said that the robbery took just three minutes and forty seconds, and that he took those particular paintings because they were nearest to the broken window. The two paintings were returned to the Van Gogh

Museum, but *View of the Sea at Scheveningen* had been damaged during the robbery and one corner of the painting was missing. Conservators used coherence tomography, a scanning technique that analyses the paint layers around the missing area, and information from photographs of the painting to recreate the section that was missing.

Van Gogh's *View of the Sea at Scheveningen*, 1882

“ The waves followed each other so quickly that ... the collision ... produced a sort of foam like drifting sand that shrouded ... the sea in a haze. ”

Vincent van Gogh

The Gates of Hell

❧

Auguste Rodin and Camile Claudel

1880–1907

W hen the sculpture student Camille Claudel started work as an assistant in the Paris studio of Auguste Rodin, regarded as the finest French sculptor of his generation, she was 19 and he 43. She soon became his lover and muse. Rodin recognized Claudel's talent, and often gave her jobs that required a great deal of skill. While working on the monumental cast for *The Gates of Hell*, a set of doors with low-relief panels, he assigned Claudel the difficult job of modelling hands and feet for some of the figures. However, he took the credit for her work, and never acknowledged the important part she played.

For years, Claudel lived in Rodin's shadow. Yet Rodin was deeply influenced by her work in bronze. Following her lead, he moved away from monumental figures to a lighter style, deftly capturing figures in movement. Their affair lasted a decade and ended when Rodin refused to leave his long-term partner, Rose Beuret. When the relationship was over, Claudel claimed that Rodin would come to her studio and steal her ideas, passing them off as his own.

Although she enjoyed a period of success, she was the victim of a society that did not approve of female artists depicting the nude. When she presented a model for a cast of a couple dancing, called *The Waltz* (1893), her patrons turned it down because the figures were naked, and she had to modify her design. At some point after 1905, she destroyed most of the work in her studio. She became increasingly reclusive, and in 1913 her brother had her committed to an asylum, where she spent the last 30 years of her life.

Long after her death, Camille Claudel finally achieved the recognition she deserved when, in 2017, her family home in Nogent-sur-Seine, southeast of Paris, opened as the Camille Claudel Museum, housing a collection of her sculptures, drawings, and designs.

Detail from a cast of Rodin's *Gates of Hell* made in1885

" Abandon all hope,
ye who enter here. "

Dante's *Inferno*, 1314

The Scream

Edvard Munch

1893

" [A] thousand thanks for the bad security. "

Note left by thieves, 1994

Thieves took just 50 seconds to steal one of the most famous modern paintings in the world, and detectives three months to find it. At 6.55 am on 12 February 1994, two men climbed a ladder to reach a window at the National Museum in Oslo. Having smashed the glass and climbed in, they took *The Scream*, painted by Norwegian artist Edvard Munch in 1893. The thieves left a note thanking the museum staff for their lax security, although they had been captured on the museum's CCTV cameras.

Munch had made two paintings of the subject, as well as two versions in pastels and several lithographs, all of which are valuable. A legitimate painting of *The Scream* would be worth around $120 million at auction, but a stolen one had no value on the open market. Norwegian police enlisted the help of the Art and Antiquities Squad of London's Metropolitan Police, who assigned detective Charles Hill to the case. Using the pseudonym Christopher Roberts, Hill contacted an art dealer suspected of having links to the thieves.

The Scream by Edvard Munch, 1893

Hill and the dealer met in a hotel in Oslo and then went to the beach resort of Åsgårdstrand to see the painting, agreeing a price of £500,000 (€600,000). Hill knew that it was the original, as wax marks caused when Munch had blown out a candle a century earlier were clearly visible. The police then arrived to retrieve the painting while Hill went for a walk. Four men were arrested and charged with the theft, though an appeals court overturned sentences against three of them on the grounds that Hill had entered Norway under a false name.

In August 2004, armed robbers in black balaclavas stole a different version of *The Scream* from the Munch Museum in Oslo, while horrified visitors watched. They also took Munch's *Madonna* (1894). Both paintings were recovered in Oslo two years later after three men were convicted of their theft. The paintings were slightly damaged, but their value had not diminished.

Portraits
of Adele

———◇———

Gustav Klimt
1907 and 1912

When visiting her aunt, Adele Bloch-Bauer, in her Vienna home in the early 1920s, the young Maria Altmann admired the paintings hanging on the walls. Little could she know that, more than 70 years later, she would be engaged in a legal battle to take ownership of the collection.

In 1907, Adele's husband, the wealthy industrialist Ferdinand Bloch-Bauer, had commissioned the Austrian artist Gustav Klimt to paint two portraits of his wife. When Adele died in 1925, she requested in her will that her husband donate the Klimt portraits to the Belvedere Gallery in Vienna, which held the national collection of Austrian art. However, Ferdinand kept the portraits.

Following the Nazi annexation of Austria in 1938, Ferdinand fled to Switzerland, leaving the paintings behind. In 1941, the regime confiscated most of his assets and art collection, and the Klimts went to the Belvedere. Ferdinand died in 1945, leaving his art collection to his nephew and two nieces, one of whom was Maria Altmann.

In 1998, the Austrian government passed a restitution law, returning art confiscated from Jewish families to its rightful owners. Altmann, who had fled to Los Angeles with her husband at the outbreak of World War II, requested the return of her uncle's paintings, including the two Klimt portraits. When the Austrian government refused, she took legal action in the US to retrieve her lawful inheritance. In 2004, the US Supreme Court upheld Maria's right to sue Austria in a US court. Given her age – Maria

Gustav Klimt's *Portrait of Adele*, 1907

❝ This is our *Mona Lisa.* ❞

Ronald S. Lauder, founder of the Neue Galerie, New York

was now 90 – she settled on arbitration, and in 2006 an Austrian court conceded that the paintings belonged to Maria Altmann and other family heirs. The family auctioned the inheritance, raising $325 million, and used a portion of it to set up the Maria Altmann Family Foundation, part of the Los Angeles Museum of the Holocaust, to commemorate Ferdinand and Adele Bloch-Bauer.

Swamp Legend

Paul Klee

1919

" To emphasize only the beautiful
seems to me to be like a mathematical
system that only concerns itself
with positive numbers. "

Paul Klee, 1906

After taking power in 1933, the Nazi regime began a purge of all modern and abstract works of art from German museums and galleries. Around 20,000 works were taken, and in July 1937, 740 of these "purged" works were put on show in Munich, in an exhibition of "Degenerate Art". They included Paul Klee's *Swamp Legend* (1919), along with works by artists such as Pablo Picasso, Henri Matisse, and Wassily Kandinsky. The purpose was to discredit and mock the art on show, and it toured 11 German and Austrian cities. In 1939, several thousand paintings were burned in Berlin. Many more were sold abroad through authorized art dealers to raise money for Germany's war effort.

One such dealer was Hildebrand Gurlitt, an art historian and gallery owner who also amassed a significant collection of his own that included works by Picasso, Matisse, Claude Monet, Marc Chagall, and Max Liebermann. Klee's *Swamp Legend*, which he bought in 1941, was among them. It remained in his collection until 1962. Gurlitt was

The Nazi Minister of Propaganda Joseph Goebbels visits the Degenerate Art exhibition in Berlin in 1935.

not alone. During World War II, auction houses and galleries across Europe dealt in stolen art. The Nazi regime pursued a policy of confiscating art of all types and from all eras in the countries it occupied. It stole from museums and churches as well as from private, mainly Jewish, owners. Its representatives sold large quantities of work in European art centres such as Paris. In 1941–42, one French auction house sold more than a million confiscated items. Other works were destined for the personal collections of Hermann Göring and Adolf Hitler, who was planning a large art museum in the Austrian city of Linz, where he had spent his youth.

The works destined for Hitler's museum were stored in a number of safe locations, including the Althaussee salt mine in Austria. When a US infantry unit arrived at the mine on 8 May 1945, following the occupation of Althaussee, it found some 12,500 items – paintings, sculptures, antiquities, books, and other works of art – including Jan and Hubert van Eyck's Ghent Altarpiece (1432)

" Colour and I are one. I am a painter. "

Paul Klee

Paul Klee's *Swamp Legend,* 1919

taken from St Bavo's Cathedral (see pages 62–63) and Michelangelo's statue *Madonna and Child* (1501–04) taken from the Church of Notre Dame in Bruges in 1944.

Some authorities estimate that the Nazis stole one-fifth of the artwork of Europe. Beginning in late 1945, the Allied governments' Monuments, Fine Arts, and Archives programme began the task of returning the art to its rightful owners. They soon discovered that many of these people had perished in Nazi death camps. However, between 1945 and 1951, an estimated 5 million items were returned. Work continued over the decades, as Jewish family members and heirs tried to reclaim plundered possessions, often unsuccessfully. The Washington Principles formulated in 1998, whereby 44 countries pledged to return works that had been looted between 1933 and 1945, were non-binding and had only limited success.

In September 2010, customs officers at the Swiss/German border questioned an elderly train passenger travelling from Zurich to Munich. The man, Cornelius Gurlitt – Hildebrand's son – was carrying €9,000 in cash, which he claimed was from the sale of an artwork in Bern. Suspecting him of tax evasion, the German police investigated his finances, and in February 2012, they discovered his father's art collection – more than 1,500 works, mostly on paper, but including some paintings. So far, only a small portion of these have been proved to be looted, but investigations continue.

And what of *Swamp Legend*? After Hildebrand Gurlitt's death in 1956, it changed hands three times between 1962 and 1988, ending up in a museum in Munich. The original owner, Sophie Lissitzky-Küppers, had moved to the Soviet Union in the 1930s, leaving her art collection with a museum in Hanover, from where the painting had been confiscated. After the war, she tried unsuccessfully to get her collection back, but died in 1978. In the 1990s, her family brought a case against the Munich museum for the return of the painting. The museum argued that it had bought the work in good faith, but after a lengthy court battle it agreed to pay an undisclosed sum to the family.

The Monuments Men

Artworks and buildings in Europe suffered wholesale destruction during World War II. In response to this, in1943, the Allied governments set up the Monuments, Fine Arts, and Archives programme, a team of art experts, academics, military, and museum personnel, to protect the treasures of Western civilization. During 1945, 345 men and women, dubbed the Monuments Men, worked alongside soldiers at the front. Risking their lives to save priceless treasures, they catalogued, photographed, and protected whatever they could, including work by Leonardo da Vinci, Rembrandt, Vermeer, and Botticelli.

Reading Girl in White and Yellow

Henri Matisse

1919

In the summer of 2013, forensics experts examining the contents of a stove in a house in the Romanian village of Caracliu found fragments of paint and canvas among the ashes. The house belonged to Olga Dogaru, whose son, Radu, was being investigated for the theft of several paintings. These included Henri Matisse's *Reading Girl in White and Yellow* (1919) from the Kunsthal museum in Rotterdam.

In 2012, the Kunsthal had celebrated its 20th anniversary by mounting an exhibition of priceless paintings, during which four thieves carried out a dawn raid, taking seven works. The thieves had entered through an emergency exit, and a CCTV recording showed that the robbery took less than two minutes. The other paintings taken were Pablo Picasso's *Harlequin Head* (1971), Claude Monet's *Waterloo Bridge* and *Charing Cross Bridge* (1901); Paul Gauguin's *Girl in Front of Open Window* (1898), Meyer de Haan's *Self-Portrait* (around 1890), and Lucian Freud's *Woman with Eyes Closed* (2002). Insurers struggled to put a price on the stolen works, but their value at auction was put at around €100 million.

Police investigators moved rapidly, and within a few months arrested and charged Radu and three other Romanian suspects. The search moved to Caracliu, where Olga Dogaru first told investigators she had buried the paintings, and then that she had burned them. As well as finding canvas fragments, the forensics team investigating her claim identified paint pigments that could have come from at least three of the paintings. The question remains: did Olga Dogaru burn all of the paintings, or might some of them turn up one day?

Myrto

Tamara de Lempicka

1929

During the Nazi occupation of Paris in World War II, a German soldier lodging in a wealthy doctor's apartment was so taken with a painting of two nude, reclining women that he took it away with him when he left. The painting, Tamara de Lempicka's *Myrto* (1929), has never been seen since.

The Polish-born De Lempicka arrived in Paris from St Petersburg in 1918. Her work was exhibited at the 1924 Salon des Femmes Artistes Modernes, and in 1925 she had her first solo show, in Milan. Her paintings, which consisted mainly of society portraits and female nudes, soon won admirers and awards, and she built up a clientele of wealthy patrons attracted by her strong Art Deco style. Among them were Dr Pierre Boucard and his wife, for whom she painted *Myrto*, one of her most celebrated lesbian paintings.

In 2018, a company that specializes in art reproductions made a full-scale facsimile of the original painting using a black-and-white photograph and matching the pigments used by De Lempicka.

Portrait of Francis Bacon

—◇—

Lucian Freud
1952

From their first meeting in the mid-1940s, British artists Francis Bacon and Lucian Freud became close friends. Both were working at the vanguard of British art, and they found stimulation in each other's company. In 1951, Freud sat for a portrait by Bacon, and the following year Bacon sat for Freud. Over the next two decades, Bacon made 16 portraits of Freud. Freud, a slower worker, made just two of Bacon and completed only one, the 1952 portrait – a small oil painting on copper measuring 18 cm by 13 cm (7 in by 5 in).

In 1988, Freud's 1952 painting of Bacon was stolen from the Neue Nationalgalerie in Berlin while on loan from London's Tate Gallery. The painting was unscrewed from the wall on a busy day in the gallery, and CCTV cameras failed to record the theft.

In 2001, Freud designed a "wanted" poster featuring the stolen portrait and offering DM300,000 (£100,000) for the painting's safe return, as he wanted to include it in a retrospective exhibition scheduled for the following year. Around 2,500 copies of the poster were printed and pasted on billboards around Berlin. The posters failed to uncover the painting, but surviving copies of the limited edition notice have become collectors' items themselves.

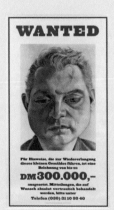

Poster advertising a reward for the safe return of Freud's portrait of Bacon.

Two Forms (Divided Circle)

Barbara Hepworth

1969

I n 2011, London's Metropolitan Police launched a new task force to combat the growing epidemic of metal theft across the city. The following day, thieves cut a valuable bronze sculpture by the British sculptor Barbara Hepworth from its plinth in London's Dulwich Park and removed it.

Two Forms (Divided Circle) had been cast in 1969, one of seven numbered editions of the statue, and placed in the park the following year. It was insured for £500,000, but the thieves probably stole it for its value as scrap metal. The sculpture has never been found, and authorities assume it was melted down and sold for a fraction of its worth.

After the theft, London-born artist Conrad Shawcross was commissioned to produce a sculpture for another site in the park. Following a public consultation, Shawcross designed Three Perpetual Chords, a series of three pieces representing musical chords. It was unveiled in 2015. Shawcross chose to use cast iron, which has little value as scrap metal, for the large, looping pieces, in the hope that they would be of no interest to thieves.

A version of Two Forms (Divided Circle) in Cambridge

Wine of Babylon

Jean-Michel Basquiat

1984

From time to time, artworks become victims of divorce settlements. On 16 April 2015, the Oscar-winning Italian film producer Vittorio Cecchi Gori accused his former wife, Croatian singer Rita Rusic, of stealing *Wine of Babylon*, painted by the American artist Jean-Michel Basquiat. Gori had purchased the work through one of his companies, G&G Productions, for $330,000 in 1988, and the couple had kept it in their Rome apartment until their divorce in 2000.

In 2013, Gori had been sentenced by an Italian court to six years in prison and ordered to pay $15.6 million to creditors of his failed production company, Safin Cinematografica. In an effort to raise funds, he decided to sell *Wine of Babylon*. But when he asked his wife for the painting, she protested that she had no idea where it was. She suggested that it may have been stolen when they sold their Rome apartment after the divorce.

Gori did not believe Rusic and sued her through G&G Productions. Later in 2015, a California court refused Gori's claim to ownership of *Wine of Babylon*, asserting that he had not filed for possession of the painting at the time of the divorce or soon enough after realizing that it was missing, even though Gori produced copies of letters that he had written to his wife in 2000 and 2009. In 2018, the court of appeal upheld the ruling that too much time had elapsed before Gori brought his case. In the meantime, the whereabouts of Basquiat's *Wine of Babylon* remain unknown.

Camouflage Series

Andy Warhol
1986

> " Art is anything you
> can get away with. "

Andy Warhol

Andy Warhol's work has long been a target for thieves. Warhol was one of the leading proponents of the 1960s' American Pop Art movement, which used mass-produced objects as subjects for art. He developed a distinctive style, combining new painting and printing techniques with witty depictions of mundane subjects. His studio in New York drew a mix of fellow artists, celebrities, and models, who were attracted by his eccentric personality as much as his art.

In early September 2009, ten silkscreen portraits of athletes were stolen overnight from the home of the collector Richard Weisman, who had tried unsuccessfully to sell them for $3 million the previous year. A year later, thieves tunnelled their way into an apartment on 9th Avenue, New York, where they helped themselves to jewellery and paintings, including a set of eight signed Warhol prints in his Camouflage Series.

On 7 April 2016, thieves broke into the Springfield Art Museum, Missouri, and stole seven of Warhol's Campbell's Soup prints, worth half a million dollars. A poster put out by the FBI to publicize the theft and appeal for information has become a downloadable artwork in itself, regarded as highly collectable by many modern art enthusiasts.

Chloe
& Emma

———◇———

Barbora Kysilkova
2013

Artists rarely get to meet the thieves who steal their work. Yet Czech-born painter Barbora Kysilkova not only met one of the men who stole two of her paintings, but subsequently painted several portraits of him.

In April 2015, petty criminal Karl-Bertil Nordland and an accomplice stole Kysilkova's *Chloe & Emma* (2013) and *Swan Song* (2013) from the Galleri Nobel in Oslo. Watching the CCTV footage some time afterwards, Kysilkova was fascinated to see how patiently the thieves removed 200 nails, taking care not to damage the canvases.

" I felt confused yet flattered. "
Barbora Kysilkova, 2020

Police apprehended the thieves, and at the court hearing Kysilkova asked Nordland why he had stolen her work. He replied that he took it because it was so beautiful, and he wanted to make her work better known – though he did not explain how he intended to do that. She then asked him to sit for her. The artist later declared that she felt great empathy for the thief and had been pleased with the compliment.

Kysilkova's partner Benjamin Ree was fascinated by the encounter, and decided to make a documentary about the theft and the relationship that subsequently developed between Kysilkova and Nordland. *The Painter and the Thief* went on to win an award at the 2020 Sundance Film Festival.

Despite her contact with Nordland, Kysilkova claims she has never been able to retrieve the two paintings and does not know of their whereabouts. However, through the loss of the works, she has been transformed from a struggling artist into a successful one.

Damaged

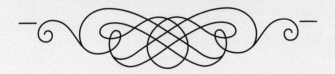

Nineveh's Lamassu

⌐——————◆——————⌐

c. 600 BCE

In 2015, Islamic State (ISIS) circulated a video on the internet showing one of its members using a pneumatic drill to deface a colossal statue of a winged bull with a human face at the site of the ancient city of Nineveh, on the outskirts of Mosul in modern Iraq. Known as lamassu, these mythical beasts were popular in ancient Mesopotamian culture. They stood guard at city and palace gates to ward off evil, and depictions abound throughout the region. The destruction of the iconic statues provoked outrage around the world.

Already a substantial settlement 3,300 years ago, Nineveh was a city in the Assyrian Empire in Mesopotamia – the expanse of land between the Euphrates and Tigris rivers, which today includes Turkey, Syria, Kuwait, Iran, and Iraq. The area gave rise to the world's first cities, its earliest written records, and complex systems of government.

The lamassu was carved from a single slab of stone 2,700 years ago, in the reign of King Sennacherib (reigned 705 BCE–681 BCE), who made Nineveh his capital. Standing 4.5 m (around 15 ft) high, it was one of a pair guarding the Nergal Gate, a ceremonial entrance to the city, and was among the few lamassu in the region still in its original position. Over the years, archaeologists have excavated and transported lamassu statues to museums abroad, including the British Museum in London, the Louvre in Paris, the National Museum of Iraq in Baghdad, the Metropolitan Museum of Art in New York, the Pergamon Museum in Berlin, and the Oriental Institute, Chicago.

When ISIS moved into the area, they destroyed the lamassu and other statues with sledgehammers and pneumatic drills, packed the site with dynamite, and filmed the detonation. Nineveh was quickly reduced to rubble. At the nearby site of Nimrod, the ziggurat (a massive stepped pyramid) was flattened with a bulldozer.

The lamassu before its destruction

" Wide spreading wings rose
above their backs, and their
breasts and bodies were profusely
adorned with curled hair. "

Sir Austen Henry Layard, 1853

ISIS has damaged or destroyed countless archaeological sites, churches, monuments, temples, and statues across the Middle East, using machine-guns, sledgehammers, axes, dynamite, and bulldozers. Their stated aim is to wipe out what it regards as idolatrous worship, but financial gain is also a driving factor. The organization regularly sells looted antiquities on the black market to raise funds to support its activities.

Other sites in the region that have been vandalized in this way include the extensive Roman city of Palmyra, an important ancient trading and cultural centre in the Syrian desert northeast of Damascus, famous for its colonnaded avenues and temples. In May 2015, ISIS militia entered the city, looting the museum and executing their enemies in front of the theatre. On 18 August, the retired head of the Antiquities Department, Khaled al-Asaad was beheaded in public for refusing to divulge the location of valuable works of art that had been removed from the site's museum for safekeeping. Some months later, the group demolished the remains of the city's ancient Roman tetrapylon, a vast pillared structure, and the theatre. Mosaics from the nearby Roman site of Apamea were excavated and sold.

It is not only the archaeological sites that have lost their treasures. The region's museums have suffered as well, and not just at the hands of ISIS. In April 2003, between the Iraqi troops of Saddam Hussein leaving Baghdad and US troops arriving, looters

The Invisible Enemy Should Not Exist

Between 2018 and 2020, Iraqi-American artist Michael Rakowitz's recreation of a lamassu occupied the Fourth Plinth in London's Trafalgar Square – a space for temporary exhibits. The colourful statue, made from 10,500 date-syrup cans, forms part of *The Invisible Enemy Should Not Exist*, Rakowitz's project to reconstruct 7,000 objects known to have been looted from the National Museum of Iraq following the US-led invasion in 2003.

A member of ISIS defaces the lamassu guarding the gate of Nineveh.

> " I find it the most iconic
> of what ISIS destroyed. "

Lamia al-Gailani Werr, Iraqi archaeologist, 2016

stole around 15,000 items from the National Museum of Iraq's Babylonian, Sumerian, and Assyrian collections. Some quick-thinking staff at the museum removed a number of objects to a secret location, but some of the oldest and most precious artefacts disappeared, including the Sumerian Warka Vase. Made of alabaster and standing at least 1 m (3 ft) high, it is more than 5,000 years old. Looters also broke apart the 4,500-year-old Golden Lyre of Ur to remove its gold inlay and gems. According to the chief investigator Matthew Bogdanos the thieves were a combination of opportunists, professional thieves, and insiders. Thanks to an amnesty, around half the objects were later recovered, with more than 700 turning up in the US and Britain. The Warka Vase was returned in the boot of a car.

Parthenon Marbles

447–432 BCE

The Parthenon stands at the centre of the Acropolis, the ancient citadel overlooking the city of Athens. Once a magnificent temple to the Greek goddess Athena Parthenos, it is a survivor of twin misfortunes – a shattering explosion in the 17th century and the wholesale looting of its ruins at the beginning of the 19th century.

The fifth-century BCE temple was built by Callicrates and Ictinus under the guidance of Phidias, the foremost sculptor of the era. Phidias also designed the marble frieze and carved relief panels, known as metopes, that decorated the building. He also carved the life-size statues of gods and legendary heroes that ranged along the pediment.

In the sixth century, the Parthenon was converted into a church, and after the Ottoman conquest of Greece in the mid-15th century, it became a mosque. In 1687, during a siege by the Venetian Republic, the Venetians bombarded the Acropolis and hit the Parthenon, where the Ottomans were storing their gunpowder. The building was severely damaged, its pillars and statues scattered all over the ground.

In 1801, Lord Thomas Bruce, seventh Earl of Elgin and the British Ambassador to the Ottoman Empire, petitioned the Ottoman authorities for permission to remove some of the sculptures. He then spent the next four years extracting about half the surviving statues, metopes, and sections of frieze, and transporting them to England.

The arrival of the Greek treasures was not universally welcomed in England, and Lord Elgin's authority to remove them was questioned. The British parliament held an enquiry in 1816, after which the government purchased the marbles from Elgin

Section of the Parthenon Marbles displayed in the British Museum

❝ They are our noblest symbol of excellence. They are a tribute to the democratic philosophy. They are our aspirations and our name. They are the essence of Greekness. **❞**

Melina Mercouri, former minister of culture, Greece

and placed them in the care of the British Museum. In 1941, the British government considered returning the marbles to Greece at the end of World War II, but they were never repatriated. With the foundation of the *International Association for the Reunification of the Parthenon Sculptures* in 2005, pressure has grown for their return to Athens, a move that the British government and the British Museum have so far resisted.

The Portland Vase

A magnificent cameo-cut glass amphora, known as the Portland Vase, survived intact for almost two millennia, passing through many owners, before being smashed to pieces by a drunken museum visitor. Dating from Roman times – the reign of Emperor Augustus – the vase is made of dark blue translucent glass, decorated with small figures in opaque white glass. It was found in a sarcophagus in the mausoleum of the Emperor Alexander Severus and his family in 1582. It passed into the collections of two cardinals, and eventually to Sir William Hamilton, the British ambassador to Naples. In the late 18th century, it was bought by the Duchess of Portland.

The vase was much admired by the 18th-century English potter Josiah Wedgwood. He produced a new line of unglazed stoneware inspired by it. In the early 19th century, the vase passed into the collection of the British Museum.

On the afternoon of 7 February 1845, William Mulcahy, from Dublin, visited the British Museum. Nobody seemed to notice his intoxicated state until he picked up a piece of basalt from another exhibit and threw it at the glass case containing the vase. The vessel shattered into some 200 pieces. John Doubleday, a restorer, made a repair that omitted 37 fragments. Meanwhile, Mulcahy was convicted of breaking the case, not the vase itself, because the offence of "wilful damage" only applied to objects up the value of £5.

The vase underwent two more restorations, in 1848 and again in 1989, when the brittle glue was replaced with resin. It is now protected by high-grade security glass.

Sutton Hoo Helmet

———◇———

Sutton Hoo Hoard

c.600 CE

In 1939, a team of archaeologists led by Basil Brown were excavating an earth mound at Sutton Hoo, in Suffolk, England, when they uncovered the outline of a ship in the ground. Within the ship was a burial chamber containing a priceless collection of gold and silver items, including armour and weapons, bowls, cups, and jewellery, that had lain in the earth for 1,400 years. The burial-ship was one of the most important hoards of Anglo-Saxon artefacts ever found, and the grave contents indicated that the occupant was probably of royal lineage, and certainly a warrior. Coins found in the area dated the burial to the first quarter of the seventh century.

Among the treasures to emerge from the soil was an exquisitely wrought metal warrior's helmet, albeit rusted and disintegrated into hundreds of tiny fragments, which were later pieced together. It may have been damaged some years after the burial, when parts of the chamber roof collapsed. Wrought from gold, silver, and other metals and decorated with garnets, the helmet consists of a series of hinged panels hanging from a flat cap beaten from a single sheet of metal. The panels depict warriors and dancers. While it resembles helmets found in similar burials from eastern Sweden, the Sutton Hoo helmet is unique in that it features a full-face panel, complete with dragons emerging from the heavy eyebrows and a decorative moustache.

Archaeologists have failed to agree on who was buried here. The leading contender is the Anglo-Saxon king Raedwald, who died around 624–625 CE and was important enough to receive such a rich burial.

Statue
of Vishnu

600 CE

In 1911, part of a seventh-century CE sandstone statue of the Hindu god Vishnu was unearthed in a cave shrine in Phnom Da, southern Cambodia. Although the statue was missing its limbs, it was bought by a Belgian collector, Adolphe Stoclet. In the 1930s, Stoclet acquired some sandstone fragments, including parts of arms and legs, feet, and a hand, that had been discovered at the same site. He hoped to use the fragments to complete his statue, but was unable to reconstruct it satisfactorily. After his death in 1973, the Cleveland Museum of Art purchased the statue and fragments. Believing that all the pieces in its possession came from a single statue, its restorers began to reconstruct it.

Using steel braces and screws, along with polyester resin (epoxy) – materials chosen for their permanency – conservators added eight fragments to the statue. When they had finished, they found they had pieces left over, including a left hand. In 2005, the museum sent the spare fragments to the National Museum of Cambodia in Phnom Penh, which had a similar Krishna torso from Phnom Da. Conservators in Phnom Penh added six of the pieces to their statue.

In 2014, a stone conservator at the Phnom Penh museum noticed that the Cleveland hand did not fit their statue properly, but it would fit onto the Cleveland statue. Using 3-D imaging, teams of conservators studied both statues to establish which fragments belonged where. Six fragments had been incorrectly attached to the Cleveland Vishnu, and two to the Phnom Penh statue. The museums then began the difficult work of undoing the reconstructions and conserving the delicate pieces of sandstone. Finally, in 2020, an exchange of fragments took place. The following year, both statues went on display in their respective museums, still incomplete but now correctly assembled.

" **When we took apart the epoxy and steel pins that held the pieces together before, we realized that some of the pieces belonged to a different sculpture.** "

Sonya Rhie Mace,
Cleveland Museum of Art

The 1978 attempt
at restoration

The Bayeux Tapestry

1070–82

History is woven into the threads of the Bayeux tapestry. More than 70 m (240 ft) in length and 50 cm (20 in) high, this vast embroidery recounts the events leading up to the Norman invasion of England in 1066, the Battle of Hastings, and the death of King Harold, in a series of scenes embroidered with woollen thread on linen panels. Despite its worn patches, frayed edges, and missing scenes, it has survived for nearly 1,000 years.

The first mention of the tapestry appears in the inventory for Bayeux Cathedral in 1476, where it was displayed above the pillars in the nave from time to time. It may have been commissioned by William the Conqueror's half-brother, Odo, who was Bishop of Bayeux, to commemorate the dedication of Bayeux cathedral in 1066. As the years passed, it was considered old-fashioned and was stored in a box in the cathedral sacristy. Local tradition has it that during the French Revolution, the tapestry was due to be cut into pieces for use as cart covers until rescued by a local offical. In 1803, at Napoleon's request, it was transported to Paris and displayed in

" It is so much about Englishness or Britishness and at the same time how that is rooted in Norman-ness. "

Simon Schama, historian, 2018

Detail of the Bayeux Tapestry

the Louvre. It was then returned to the town of Bayeux, where a curator at the town hall would show it to visitors by unwinding it from a huge spindle and winding it up again, damaging the edges. The tapestry is now kept in the Bayeux Museum.

It is not known if the tapestry was embroidered in Normandy or England. Some authorities say that it was made by the ladies of the court of Matilda, wife of William the Conqueror; others that it was sewn by unknown workers in Canterbury. Either way, it is surprising that this vast example of medieval embroidery has survived for so long.

Frescoes of the Lives of St Francis and the Saints

Giotto

c.1300

" The history of medieval art
passes through this building. **"**

Sergio Fusetti, art restorer, 1999

Fresco depicting St Francis, Sant'Agostino church, Assisi

At 2.30 am on 26 September 1997, an earthquake measuring 5.1 on the Richter scale struck the Umbrian hillside town of Assisi. The following morning, a small group of friars, engineers, and journalists entered the upper church of the town's 13th-century basilica. As they inspected the damage, a second, more forceful, quake struck. Within moments, sections of the walls and vaulted ceiling around the entrance collapsed, killing two friars and two engineers.

The basilica, built over the tomb of St Francis of Assisi, consists of an upper and a lower church. Several of the greatest artists of the late Gothic and early Renaissance periods, including Cimabue, Simone Martini, and Giotto di Bondone, decorated both churches. The 28 scenes in the fresco cycle of the Life of St Francis by Giotto and his workshop covered the area inside the entrance to the upper church.

After the earthquake, restorers used computers to separate and grade the frescoes' surviving fragments by colour and filled in the blank patches with pigments of similar hues. Two years after their destruction, most of the frescoes had been restored.

Pietà

———◇———

Michelangelo

1499

On 21 May 1972, a visitor to St Peter's Basilica in Rome entered a side chapel, vaulted over an altar rail, and violently attacked Michelangelo's *Pietà* with a hammer, hitting it several times, while shouting "I am Jesus Christ". It was Whit Sunday and the basilica was full of visitors, who pulled away the attacker, Hungarian-born Laszlo Toth, and wrestled him to the ground.

The *Pietà* depicts the Virgin Mary cradling the body of the dead Christ. Toth had severely damaged it. The Virgin's nose and eye were badly disfigured, the left arm was broken at the elbow,

> **❝** Every block of stone has a statue inside it and it is the task of the sculptor to discover it. **❞**
>
> **Michelangelo**

Michelangelo's *Pietà*, St Peter's, Rome

and around 100 fragments of marble lay on the floor. Toth was arrested and committed to a psychiatric hospital for two years. He was then deported.

The *Pietà*, which Michelangelo carved from a single block of Carrara marble, is renowned for its lifelike qualities. The 16th-century biographer Giorgio Vasari said of it, "It is a miracle that a rock, which before was without form, can take on such perfection that even nature sometimes struggles to create in the flesh." Art restorers were divided about what form the restoration work should take. Some thought the statue should not be repaired, to reflect the violence of current times. Others thought that the repair lines marking the damaged areas should be clear to viewers. In the end, the Vatican decided on an "integral restoration" – one that would not be visible to the naked eye.

Restorers spent five months identifying all the fragments that had been recovered. They then began to piece the statue back together, working in situ in the chapel so that it would not have to be moved. They mixed specially prepared glue with Carrara marble dust to fix the fragments back in place, producing repairs that are almost invisible. They removed a small piece from the back of the statue and carved a new nose identical to the original, using photographs taken before the attack as a reference. Ten months later, the *Pietà* went back on display. To protect it from further attacks, a large bulletproof glass screen was installed in front of the statue.

According to Vasari in his *Life of Michelangelo*, the young sculptor overheard a visitor in St Peter's attribute his *Pietà* to the artist Cristoforo Solari. Michelangelo was so incensed that he stayed overnight to chisel the words "*Michael a[n]gelus Bonarotus Florent[inus] Facieba[t]*" – "Michelangelo Buonarotti of Florence made me" – across the Virgin's body, an action he immediately regretted, according to Vasari. The *Pietà* is Michelangelo's only signed work.

Michelangelo's Florence *Pietà* (known as the *Bandini Pietà*), a group of four figures – the dead Christ, Mary Magdalene, the Virgin Mary, and Nicodemus, who helped prepare Christ's body for burial – was another of his statues to suffer damage. Michelangelo spent eight years working on the *Bandini Pietà*, beginning in 1547, when he was in his seventies, and gave the figure of Nicodemus his own features, perhaps because the statue was intended for Michelangelo's own tomb. But by 1555, the Virgin's hand had broken off and the statue had lost several limbs,

Shooting at art

In July 1987, a man called Robert Cambridge entered the National Gallery in London. Standing in front of Leonardo da Vinci's drawing *The Virgin and Child with St Anne and St John the Baptist*, he pulled out a sawn-off shotgun and fired at it, shattering the glass case. Shards of glass damaged a small area of the drawing. Cambridge later told police that he had wanted to protest at the "political, social, and economic conditions in Britain". Restoration of the drawing took a year to complete. Cambridge was committed to a psychiatric institution.

> ❝ The *Bandini Pietà* is a true masterpiece that reflects the tormented soul of the great genius Michelangelo. ❞

Simonetta Brandolini D'Adda, Friends of Florence Foundation, 2021

and Michelangelo abandoned the work. He gave the damaged statue to his servant, who hired another sculptor to repair it, before selling it to a Roman banker, Francesco Bandini, who placed it in his garden.

It used to be assumed that Michelangelo destroyed the *Bandini Pietà* himself, possibly out of frustration, but new research throws doubt on the theory. In 2021, restorers at the Opera del Duomo Museum in Florence, which houses the work, finished a two-year restoration project, during which they made important discoveries. The marble turned out not to be from Carrara, but a harder kind that would have been difficult to carve. It also contained little veins that were not visible on the surface. While these factors may have led Michelangelo to attack the statue in frustration, the restorers failed to find marks to indicate that this had been the case.

Michelangelo's *Bandini Pietà*

The Night Watch

Rembrandt van Rijn

1642

I n a bizarre act of artistic vandalism, Rembrandt van Rijn's monumental canvas *The Night Watch* (1642) was cut down in size to fit a space on the wall of Amsterdam's Town Hall. The painting had originally hung in the banqueting hall, but was transferred to the Town Hall in 1715.

Rembrandt was commissioned in 1639 by Captain Frans Banning Cocq, commander of Amsterdam's civic guard, to paint a group portrait of 34 officers and guardsmen to hang in the banqueting hall of the Kloveniersdoelen (Musketeers' Meeting Hall). As was common practice, the men represented in the painting paid an upfront fee to offset the expense of the commission. This was 90 guilders each on average, although a prominent position in the painting would have cost more.

When the painting arrived in the Town Hall, workmen had to cut strips off the canvas in order to fit it into its allotted space. Pieces about 60 cm (2 ft) wide were cut from the left side – removing two

> **❝** It is thanks to artificial intelligence that we can so closely simulate the original painting and the impression it would have made. **❞**
>
> **Robert Erdmann**, Rijksmuseum

Rembrandt's *The Night Watch*, 1642, after it was reduced in size

figures – and the top edge, and narrower pieces were cut from the bottom edge and the right side, reducing the painting to 3.8 m high by 4.5 m wide (12 ft by 14 ft). The discarded pieces were most likely thrown out or destroyed.

By good fortune, in around 1650, the Dutch genre-scene painter Gerrit Lundens had painted a copy of the work, and in 2019, restorers at the Rijksmuseum used this and computer-generated images to make a copy of the missing portions. In 2021, the complete painting was temporarily reconstructed and placed on view for three months, revealing the two missing figures on the left-hand side.

The Rokeby Venus

Diego Velázquez
c.1647–51

The Rokeby Venus, by Diego Velázquez, 1754

In March 1914, a young Canadian woman entered the National Gallery in London and made her way to the room where a portrait of Venus was on display. She took out a meat cleaver from under her jacket and lunged at the canvas, slashing it several times before she was overpowered by guards. What provoked Ontario-born Mary Richardson to attack *The Rokeby Venus* – a painting by the Spanish artist Diego Velázquez from the mid-17th century?

" I have tried to destroy the picture of the most beautiful woman in mythological history as a protest against the Government for destroying Mrs Pankhurst, who is the most beautiful character in modern history. "

Mary Richardson, 1914

Richardson was a member of the Women's Social and Political Union, founded in 1903 and better known as the Suffragette Movement. Members undertook increasingly violent acts of civil disobedience to draw attention to the inequality between men and women in British society, particularly women's lack of the right to vote in parliamentary elections. Richardson was arrested after the attack and sentenced to six months in prison. She later explained that her actions had been inspired by the government's treatment of the founder of the Women's Social and Political Union, Emmeline Pankhurst. At the time, Pankhurst was being force-fed in prison.

The Rokeby Venus was a popular exhibit at the National Gallery, valued at around £45,000 in 1906. Velázquez had produced the painting, originally known as *The Toilet of Venus,* for the Spanish royal court. It was smuggled from Spain to England in 1813, during the Napoleonic Wars, and later entered the collection at Rokeby Park in Yorkshire. In 1906, it was purchased by public subscription and exhibited at the National Gallery in London. Some 30,000 visitors admired the painting in the first year alone.

After the attack by Richardson, the National Gallery's chief restorer, Helmut Ruhemann, repaired the painting. Richardson was vilified in the press and received little sympathy from the British public. Nonetheless, six years later, in 1918, some British women won voting rights and the right to stand for election to parliament. In 1928, all British women obtained the same voting rights as men.

The Dream

Pablo Picasso

1932

" At that moment, his elbow
crashed backward right
through the canvas.
There was a terrible noise. "

Nora Ephron

DAMAGED

Handling a valuable painting can have expensive consequences, as Las Vegas casino owner Steve Wynn found out in 2006. At the time, Wynn was the owner of Pablo Picasso's *The Dream* (*Le Rêve*), and had agreed to sell it to American hedge-fund manager and art collector Steve Cohen for $139 million. But before they had concluded the deal, Wynn accidentally put his elbow through the canvas while showing it to some friends, including the writer Nora Ephron, creating a rip in the figure's left forearm.

Picasso painted *The Dream*, a portrait of his lover, Marie-Thérèse Walter, in 1932. In 1941, it was bought by American art collectors Victor and Sally Ganz for $7,000. After their death, their family sold much of their art collection to pay inheritance tax. Picasso's *Le Rêve* fetched $48.4 million. The buyer, Austrian hedge fund manager Wolfgang Flöttl, sold it to Wynn in 2001 for $60 million.

After damaging the painting so catastrophically, Wynn released Cohen from their agreement and had it restored. The 5 cm (2 in) tear, which allegedly cost $110,000 to repair, dramatically reduced the value

Picasso's *The Dream*, 1932

of the painting, although Wynn was assured that it was still worth at least $80 million. He filed a claim with his insurers, Lloyds of London, to make up the lost value. When the insurers refused the claim, Wynn sued. Three months later, the claim was settled for an undisclosed sum.

Cohen was still determined to own *The Dream*, and in 2013 he purchased it from Wynn for $155 million, the highest amount to date paid by a US private collector for a piece of art.

Yellow Pumpkin

—◇—

Yayoi Kusama

1994

In 1994, the Japanese artist Yayoi Kusama installed a 1.8-m- (6-ft-) high fibreglass pumpkin on the pier on Naoshima, an island famous for its large collection of modern art. On 9 August 2021, a typhoon struck the island, and the sculpture was swept into the sea. It was buffeted by the waves for several hours until the storm died down and the damaged artwork could be retrieved from the water and repaired.

Kusama has been fascinated by pumpkins since childhood, and they were among the first objects that she drew. She began featuring them in her work in 1946, and has continued to represent the form in a variety of materials, shapes, textures, and colours ever since. The pumpkin became a trademark of Kusama's art, and

> **" Kusama's Pumpkin ... continuously changes the everyday landscape into something new. "**
>
> **Benesse Art Site's magazine**

Yayoi Kusama's *Yellow Pumpkin* sculpture before it was swept into the sea

inspired *Yellow Pumpkin* (1994), her largest single piece. The bright yellow form is covered with black dots of varying sizes arranged in a symmetrical design.

The destruction of her work was not new to Kusama. When she moved from Japan to New York, she took very few paintings and drawings with her and destroyed the work kept at her parents' house before leaving. Her mother had always opposed her artistic ambitions.

Niagara Falls

Valerie Hegarty

2007

" It doesn't just depict an
experience, but instead, actually
goes through an experience. **"**

Valerie Hegarty, 2008

C reated from wood, foam board, paint, gel, and glue by the
American artist Valerie Hegarty, *Niagara Falls* puts a smile on
the face of every viewer. The subject is the famous waterfall on the
Niagara River, straddling the border between the US and Canada.
For centuries, people have been attracted to the site, drawn by the
power of the water and the spectacular optical effects it produces.

Valerie Hegarty's *Niagara Falls*, 2007

At first glance, the work looks like a conventional framed painting that has been badly damaged. But in this case the damage is deliberate. Hegarty broke the frame on one side and twisted it so that it curves in on itself. The lower left corner of the painting looks as if it has been almost devoured by fire, while the water appears to pour out of the frame, thus extinguishing the flames. Much of Hegarty's work represents stages of destruction, acknowledging that artworks are not immortal, and succumb to damage or the degradation of the elements.

Cracked Canyon, also dating from 2007, is another visual pun. Here Hegarty uses a framed painting of a canyon hung on a wall. The wall has a large crack running from ceiling to floor. The frame is broken in exactly the same place as the wall, and the canvas is damaged along the same line. A few flakes of plaster from the wall lie on the ground. It takes a moment or two for the viewer to make sense of it.

Destroyed

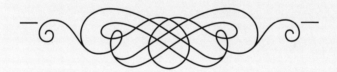

The Buddhas of Bamiyan

544 CE

> " The Creator gives divine
> inspiration to His subjects
> to make such wonders. "
>
> **Zakaria al-Qazwini**, 13th century

For around 1,500 years, two giant statues of the Buddha – the largest standing Buddhas in the world – stood beside the Silk Road trade route through Afghanistan. Carved into the face of a cliff in the Bamiyan valley during the sixth and early seventh centuries, when the area was a busy trade hub and a centre of Buddhism, the two statues stood 53 m (175 ft) and about 40 m (120 ft) high respectively. Buddhist monks lived in small caves carved into the mountainside around the figures, welcoming passing travellers. Several of the caves were painted with scenes from the Buddha's life.

In February 2001, Afghanistan's Taliban government announced its intention to destroy the Buddhist statues, which it condemned as idols. Having gained the attention of the world's media, in March, fighters packed the crevices around the statues with explosives and detonated them. The massive figures did not collapse immediately, so the militants added more explosives and rockets.

One of the two Buddhas before it was targeted by the Taliban

The figures were destroyed to such an extent that they cannot be rebuilt. Today, empty niches in the rock face mark the spot where they once stood. There is nothing remaining, apart from photographs of the statues and a video showing the moment when the dynamite was detonated.

The Justice of Trajan and Herkinbald

Rogier van der Weyden

1435–50

" Master Rogier, the famous
painter ... So skilled were you at
rendering the shape of things,
Brussels mourns over your death. "

The epitaph on Rogier van der Weyden's gravestone

ogier van der Weyden's *The Justice of Trajan and Herkinbald*, a set of four panels in Brussels town hall, was considered to be a masterpiece. Albrecht Dürer, one of the greatest German Renaissance artists, was among those who came simply to admire it, and several artists made copies of the paintings. Then, between 13 and 15 August 1695, French troops invaded Brussels and set much of the city ablaze. Among the casualties was the town hall, which burned to the ground. *The Justice of Trajan and Herkinbald* perished in the flames.

The most celebrated of Van der Weyden's monumental oil paintings, the set of four panels depicted scenes from the lives of the second-century Roman emperor Trajan and the legendary 12th-century Duke Herkinbald of Brabant. Measuring some 4 m (12 ft) high and with a span of about 10 m (30 ft), they adorned the town hall's Golden Chamber. The panel's themes of justice and impartiality were particularly suitable for a room in which criminal cases were heard.

By good luck, we know what the original looked like, because in the same year that the Justice panels were hung in the Golden Chamber, a tapestry based on them was completed. George of Saluzzo, wanting to celebrate his nomination as bishop of the Swiss diocese of Lausanne in 1440, obtained drawings of Van der Weyden's great work. No one knows if Van der Weyden was aware of the tapestry, or whether he supplied the drawings. Fortunately, the tapestry has survived and today hangs in the Bern Historical Museum in Switzerland. It is a reminder that an estimated three-quarters of all works by the great artists of the past have been lost.

Tapestry copy of one of the painting's panels

Bonfire
of the Vanities

◇

1497

On 7 February 1497, the Dominican friar Girolomo Savonarola summoned the citizens of Florence to the city's main square and urged them to throw their possessions onto a huge bonfire. Among those who attended was Sandro Botticelli, one of the greatest artists of the age, and a favourite of the powerful Medici family.

For years, Savonarola had been preaching sermons attacking the corruption of the Church and urging the people of Florence to embrace an austere way of life. He exhorted them to burn all "lascivious" images and railed against the Medici family for commissioning pagan works of art and books. At a series of fires in front of the town hall, his followers piled up "vanities" for burning – rich clothes and fabrics, cosmetics, perfumes, and mirrors, together with paintings, tapestries, furniture, musical instruments, and books. There are no records of what was destroyed, but there is little doubt that some of the finest works of the Renaissance went up in flames. According to the 16th-century biographer Giorgio Vasari, Botticelli was sympathetic to Savonarola's views, though not a follower, and threw some of his own paintings – those with pagan themes – into the flames.

Nineteenth-century illustration of Florence's Bonfire of the Vanities

" God must not find the house
sullied by vile things, but tidy and
devoid of any earthly affection. "

Girolomo Savonarola

Another disaster in Florence, nearly 500 years later, was even more destructive. On the night of 3 November 1966, after days of persistent rain, rising waters burst the Levane and La Penna dams, causing the banks of the River Arno to overflow. In the worst flood since 1557, water swirled through buildings and churches, destroying frescoes and painted panels, and depositing more than half a billion tonnes of silt. Volunteers from all over Italy, dubbed the "Mud Angels", set about rescuing what they could, but some 14,000 artefacts were badly damaged or destroyed, while millions of books were ruined by damp.

Equestrian Portrait of Emperor Philip IV

Peter Paul Rubens

c.1628

Soon after midnight on Christmas Eve, 1734, the chapel bells of the Royal Alcázar in Madrid began to ring. They were not a call to Mass, as was originally assumed, but a warning that fire had broken out in the palace. As the commotion spread, the main entrance gates of the palace were locked to prevent looting. As a result, hundreds of works of art in the Spanish royal collection were destroyed in the ensuing conflagration, including paintings by the Flemish artist Peter Paul Rubens, Titian, and other masters of the Renaissance and Baroque eras.

Locking the palace gates also prevented fire fighters gaining access to the royal residence. As flames swept through the galleries, staff tried to rescue whatever they could, taking vast canvases down from the walls and throwing them out of the windows. Peter Paul Rubens' *Equestrian Portrait of Emperor Philip IV* (c.1628) was destroyed, as were several paintings by the 16th-century Venetian artist Titian, including all 11 in his Roman Emperors series. Philip IV's court painter Diego Velázquez's monumental canvas *The Expulsion of the Moriscos* (c.1627) was also consumed by fire, along with his *Venus and Adonis* (c.1659). Paintings by Leonardo da Vinci, Albrecht Dürer, Raphael, Tintoretto, Veronese, and El Greco were also burnt.

" Here I keep to painting, as I do
everywhere, and already I have done
the equestrian portrait of His Majesty,
to his great pleasure and satisfaction. "

Peter Paul Rubens, 1628

" Reality and metaphor, the Alcazar fire changed the urban profile of the capital of the Bourbons. "

María Victoria López-Cordón

The Alcazar in the 18th century

However, some paintings were saved. Titian's large equestrian portrait, *Emperor Charles V at Mühlberg* (1548), survived. Velázquez's *Las Meninas* (1656), the large group portrait of the Infanta and her ladies-in-waiting, was cut from its frame and dropped from an upper gallery. Although damaged, it also survived.

Four days passed before the fire was finally extinguished. By that time, almost all the furniture had been destroyed, and several surviving canvases had suffered severe water damage in the unsuccessful efforts to save the building. Nobody established how the fire had started, although rumours circulated that the cause may have been an unattended oil lamp in the studio of the royal portraitist, Jean Ranc. The destruction could have been worse. Some weeks earlier, the king had ordered the removal of part of the Royal Collection to the newly refurbished Buen Retiro Palace in Madrid. Despite that, more than 500 canvases were destroyed.

In the case of Rubens' *Equestrian Portrait of Emperor Philip IV*, the painting was not lost without a trace. As was common practice among the court artists of the time, soon after Rubens completed the royal portrait, Velázquez and his assistants had made a copy – known as a "diplomatic" painting. This now hangs in the Uffizi Galleries in Florence.

Windsor Castle fire

A valuable collection amassed over a thousand years narrowly avoided destruction when fire ripped through 100 rooms at Windsor Castle in November 1992. On the morning of 20 November, a spotlight bulb set a curtain ablaze in Queen Victoria's Private Chapel. From there, the flames spread into the adjacent St George's Hall. Despite the efforts of firefighters, the blaze raged for 15 hours. While the interiors were severely damaged, only one painting, *George III Reviewing the Troops* by the English portraitist William Beechey, was destroyed.

The Amber Room

In 1941, one of the most sumptuous rooms that ever existed, the Amber Room in the Catherine Palace at Tsarskoye Selo, near St Petersburg, vanished in the fog of World War II. Lined with amber panels and carved decorations, the room had been called "the Eighth Wonder of the World". By day, visitors were enthralled by the amber's subtle hues; at night, the panels reflected the light from 565 candles.

Popularly known as the "gold of the North", amber is a fossilized tree resin found along the Baltic Sea, and highly valued for its rich golden colour and translucency. The room's first amber panels were given by King Frederick of Prussia to the Russian emperor Peter the Great, in 1716. Peter's daughter Elizabeth commissioned additional panels in 1743 and had them all installed in a room in the Catherine Palace. Catherine the Great added further panels in the 1760s.

A reproduction of the Amber Room, installed at the Catherine Palace in 2003

" The eye ... is amazed and is
blinded by the wealth and warmth
of tints, representing all colours
of the spectrum. "

Théophile Gautier, 1866

When the German army entered St Petersburg in October 1941, soldiers packed the panels into 27 crates for removal to Germany. The crates were taken to Königsberg (now Kaliningrad in Russia) and placed in the castle museum. In 1944, the British air force bombed Königsberg, and when the Red Army captured the city in April 1945, the amber was nowhere to be found. The fate of the panels remains a mystery. Did they go up in flames in the air raid? One theory is that they were shipwrecked on the Baltic Sea while being moved to another location.

In 2003, the Soviet and German governments completed a joint project to create a replica of the room at the Catherine Palace. Today, visitors can again experience the glory of the Amber Room.

The Last Moments of Michel Lepeletier

Jacques-Louis David

1793

" The artist must be a philosopher ... an artistic genius should have no other guide except the torch of reason. "

Jacques-Louis David

An engraving of Jacques-Louis David's lost painting of Lepeletier

J acques-Louis David, the greatest French painter of his day, was an anti-Royalist during the French Revolution (1789–99). He painted the death scenes of two revolutionary leaders, Louis-Michel Lepeletier and Jean-Paul Marat, both of whom were assassinated. While the painting of Marat survived, the one of Lepeletier was destroyed.

One of the most influential leaders of the movement for reform, Lepeletier was elected president of France's new National Constituent Assembly in 1790. Three years later, he cast one of the decisive votes that led to the execution of Louis XVI and his family. On the day before the execution, a member of the Garde du Corps, the king's bodyguard, assassinated Lepeletier using a sabre. David painted the revolutionary's dying moments, depicting Lepeletier lying on pillows, the bleeding wound caused by the blade visible below his ribcage. David followed this with *The Death of Marat* (1793). Marat was assassinated in his bath tub by Charlotte Corday, a political opponent.

After David's death in Brussels in 1825, *The Last Moments of Michel Lepeletier*, along with preparatory drawings, passed into the possession of Lepeletier's daughter, Louise, who decided to destroy the work. However, one of David's pupils engraved a copy of *The Last Moments of Michel Lepeletier* and that has survived.

THE LAST MOMENTS OF MICHEL LEPELETIER

Religion
Attended by
the Virtues

———◊———

Angelica Kauffman

c.1800

A chalk drawing in the British Royal Collection and an engraving made in 1812 by William Henry Worthington are the only records of Angelica Kauffman's monumental painting *Religion Attended by the Virtues*, painted between 1800 and 1807, and destroyed in a bombing raid in 1941. They offer tantalizing glimpses of the work that was hailed as Kauffman's greatest triumph.

" The whole world is Angelica–mad. "

Engraver, c.1770s

Born in Switzerland, Kauffman divided her time between Italy and London. She was highly regarded by her contemporaries. In 1768, she and Mary Moser were the only female founding members of the Royal Academy of Arts in London.

Kauffman specialized in allegorical and history paintings, as well as portraits for wealthy clients. *Religion Attended by the Virtues* was her largest and most ambitious canvas, measuring 2.1 m by 2.7 m (7 ft by 9 ft) and featuring 11 life-size figures. It was first owned by James

Forbes, who bequeathed it to the British Museum in 1835. The painting was transferred to the newly formed National Gallery three years later, becoming one of the first pieces in the British national collection. The canvas was later transferred to the Tate Gallery. In 1913, it was sent to Plymouth in southwest England, where it was installed in the Guildhall.

Plymouth was bombed during World War II, and it is presumed that the painting was destroyed in a raid in March 1941, as it has not been seen since. No records of the painting survive, although a pre-War photograph shows it hanging in the building. In 2018, the Tate launched a public appeal in the hope that Kauffman's masterpiece might have been rescued and may still be hidden away somewhere.

Angelica Kauffman's *Religion Attended by the Virtues, c.*1800

The Stone Breakers

Gustave Courbet

1849

B etween 13 and 15 February 1945, during the final stages of World War II, Allied bombers blitzed the German city of Dresden. Over three days and nights, British and US planes carried out four raids, dropping close to 4,000 tonnes (3,900 tons) of explosives. Within days, the city was reduced to ruins, its buildings destroyed by explosives and fire. At least 25,000 people are thought to have been killed in the attack.

Even as the city, which was known for its beauty and artistic treasures, was being bombarded, German troops hurriedly packed artworks from the city's galleries and museums onto trucks to ferry them to safety in the nearby fortress of Königstein. Despite this precaution, some 154 paintings were destroyed on the way to the

> **"** *The Stone Breakers* ... challenged convention by rendering scenes from daily life on the large scale previously reserved for history painting and in an emphatically realistic style. **"**
>
> **Kathryn Calley Galitz**, Metropolitan Museum of Art, 2009

The Stone Breakers by Gustave Courbet, 1849

fortress. Among them was a monumental canvas painted in 1849 by French artist Gustave Courbet. *The Stone Breakers*, measuring 1.6 m by 2.6 m (5 ft 5 in by 8 ft 5 in), featured two labourers engaged in the gruelling task of breaking up rocks. A young man lifts a large boulder while an old man smashes pieces of rock with a hammer.

The painting's subject matter was novel for mid-19th century French art. Most painters depicted epic historical events, whereas Courbet, who urged fellow artists to paint what was real, showed ordinary labourers engaged in heavy work. Karl Marx and Friedrich Engels had published *A Communist Manifesto* just a year earlier, and revolutionary ideas were spreading throughout Europe. Courbet's work reflected the changing times. In addition, his handling of the paint is deliberately rough and unfinished, reflecting the hardships and deprivation suffered by the two men. Today, all that survives of Courbet's revolutionary painting is a colour photograph taken before *The Stone Breakers* was destroyed.

Washington Crossing the Delaware

Emanuel Gottlieb Leutze

1850

The second version of *Washington Crossing the Delaware,* 1850

❝ The painting has become, over
the years, the very emblem of
patriotism for Americans. **❞**

Professor Barbara Groseclose, Ohio State University

On the night of 25 December 1776, General George Washington and his troops crossed the Delaware River some 14 km (9 miles) north of Trenton, New Jersey, and surprised Hessian soldiers fighting for the British. Washington's soldiers captured more than 1,000 Hessians and killed 22 in the encounter. The most memorable image of this turning point in the American War for Independence, *Washington Crossing the Delaware*, was produced by Emanuel Gottlieb Leutze, a German artist living in Düsseldorf. The monumental canvas shows a resolute Washington at the front of a flotilla of wooden rowing boats as they cut through the icy waters of the Delaware. The breadth of the river in the painting, and the number of men crammed into the tiny boats, owe a good deal to poetic licence.

Leutze was born in Germany in 1816, and his family emigrated to the US in 1825. He showed artistic talent as a young boy, and at the age of 24 returned to Germany to study art in Düsseldorf. Following the collapse of a series of revolutions in Europe in 1848, Leutze turned to America for inspiration. He completed the canvas recording Washington's victory at the Delaware in 1850, but it was damaged in a fire at his studio. He was able to repair the canvas, and it was later acquired by the Kunsthalle in Bremen. The canvas was widely admired by generations of Germans until it was destroyed by Allied bombing during World War II.

Some months after he had finished the original painting, Leutze made a copy. It was commissioned by the French art dealer Adolphe Goupil, who put it on display in his Broadway showrooms in New York City in October 1851. The painting was purchased by Marshall O. Roberts, a wealthy art collector, for the sum of $10,000. In 1897, this second version of *Washington Crossing the Delaware* was donated to the newly established Metropolitan Museum of Art in New York, where it hangs today.

Beneath The Blue Room

Picasso

1901

I n 2014, a team of conservators from Cornell University, the National Gallery in Washington, D.C., and the Winterthur Museum in Delaware, examined Picasso's *The Blue Room* (1901), owned by the Philips Collection in Washington, using X-ray imaging techniques. Their suspicions were confirmed. Another work by Picasso, a portrait of a bearded man, lay underneath *The Blue Room*. In common with many artists, Picasso had destroyed his own work by painting over it.

Picasso completed *The Blue Room*, a study of a young woman standing in a large tub, when he was 19, shortly after he had arrived in Paris from Barcelona. It was a period of intense activity

" When he [Picasso] had an idea ... he just had to get it down and realize it. "

Susan Behrends Frank, curator, 2014

for the young artist. If he was dissatisfied with a painting, or had a new idea, he would sometimes take a canvas he had already used and paint over the existing image. Good quality paint and canvas were expensive, and he may have done this to save money, or it may have been his way of moving his work forward during a time of rapid artistic development.

Art experts had long suspected that Picasso reused canvases, but they had no means of verifying their suspicions until infrared and X-ray imaging techniques were developed for seeing beneath the surface of oil paintings. In the case of the bearded man, the portrait appeared not to be an abandoned sketch but a finished work. The identity of the man, who is seated with his head resting on his hand, has yet to be established.

Art historians and restorers use X-ray imaging not only to view beneath the surface of a painting, but also to analyse paintings. This is useful for restoration and to establish that a painting is genuine by revealing the artist's idiosyncratic techniques and the provenance of the pigments used.

The Blue Room, by Pablo Picasso

Water Lilies

—◇—

Claude Monet

1914–26

On the afternoon of 15 April 1958, traffic came to a halt on New York's Fifth Avenue. Onlookers gazed in horror as one of the city's most prestigious museums was engulfed in flames. Scores of firefighters fought the blaze, which had broken out shortly after noon in the Museum of Modern Art. As the building was evacuated, windows shattered, shards of glass landing on the street below.

Despite the suffocating heat, several survivors, including the chairman of the museum's board, Nelson Rockefeller, returned to the burning building to rescue the artworks. Forensic scientists believed that the fire was started by a cigarette butt discarded by a maintenance worker.

> **"** Poetry in paint was consumed yesterday when Claude Monet's huge painting of water lilies perished in the fire at the Museum of Modern Art. **"**

The New York Times, 1958

Many portable works were salvaged, but a huge oil painting titled *Water Lilies*, measuring 5.6 m (18½ ft) long, by the French Impressionist Claude Monet perished. A smaller (2-m-/7-ft-wide) *Water Lilies* painting was badly damaged. Following the fire, the Museum of Modern Art donated the smaller, blackened canvas to New York University's Conservation Clinic.

Among the hundreds of paintings of his gardens at Giverny, Monet produced 40 large-scale panels of the lily ponds. He had moved into his house in Giverny, northwest of Paris in 1883 and spent the next 30 years painting the gardens there. The Museum of Modern Art acquired its *Water Lilies* panel in 1955 and the smaller painting a year later.

In 2017, Factum Arte, a company specializing in digital reproductions of lost or damaged works of art, made a copy of Monet's smaller work based on a 1956 black-and-white photograph. The technicians studied other *Water Lilies* canvases in order to reproduce the colours exactly.

Factum Arte's copy of the smaller *Water Lilies* painting lost in the fire

Man at the Crossroads

Diego Rivera

1933

I n January 1932, Nelson Rockefeller, son of American oil magnate John D. Rockefeller, commissioned the Mexican artist Diego Rivera to paint a mural in the lobby of 30 Rockefeller Plaza, part of the Rockefeller Center in New York. The title suggested for the work was *Man at the Crossroads Looking with Hope and High Vision to the Choosing of a New and Better Future.* Within a year of its completion, the mural had been destroyed, a victim of political censorship.

Rockefeller knew that Rivera was a former member of the Communist Party, but he wanted the work to show how capitalism and socialism could flourish together. He approved the preparatory sketch, and work began in March 1933. At the centre of the main panel, Rivera placed a man operating machinery, highlighting the achievements of the modern era. More controversially, he also included a portrait of the Russian leader Vladimir Lenin, which had not been in the sketch.

" Rivera paints Scenes of Communist Activity and John D. Jr. Foots the Bill. "

The New York World Telegram

Recreated section of Diego Rivera's *Man at the Crossroads* depicting Lenin

When Rockefeller was informed about the inclusion of the figure of Lenin, he asked Rivera to remove it. Rivera replied that the portrait was essential to the work, and suggested adding in Abraham Lincoln as well. By now the dispute had reached the newspapers, which took Rockefeller's side, and work on the mural came to a halt. Artists sided with Rivera, while the Rockefeller family were anxious not to offend the American government by including what looked like Soviet propaganda.

Unable to complete the mural, Rivera returned to Mexico in late 1933, where he agreed to paint a scaled-down version of the work in the Palacio de Bellas Artes in Mexico City.

In February 1934, the Rockefeller Center Corporation ordered that the mural be plastered over. Today, only a few black-and-white photographs remain of the masterpiece.

Three Works

❦

Käthe Kollwitz

1905, 1910

In 2017, the Dresden Kupferstich-Kabinett (Collection of Prints, Drawings, and Photographs) was preparing an exhibition of the work of the German artist Käthe Kollwitz. Not long before the exhibition opened, the museum received three Kollwitz prints, believed lost since World War II, from the Finnish art authorities. The prints – a lithograph and two etchings – featured two female heads and a self-portrait. Prior to the war, they had been part of the Kupferstich-Kabinett's collection of Kollwitz's work, which dates back to 1898.

Nothing is known about the prints' disappearance from the museum, but it most likely took place during a period of looting at the end of the war. Then, in the 1970s, the prints were confiscated by Helsinki customs officers, who sent them to the National Board of Antiquities, not knowing who they were by. Nobody at the Board was able to identify the works, and they were placed in a filing cabinet labelled "anonymous".

In 2017, curators carrying out a review of old materials in the board's archives recognized Kollwitz's stamp and old catalogue numbers. The German artist had lived through a period of social unrest and extraordinary violence, including two world wars. Her work, mostly sculptures, woodcuts, and lithographs, depicted the

Self-portrait with Hand on Forehead (1910), one of the lost prints by Käthe Kollwitz

horrors of war and the profound suffering humans inflict on each other. Of the three works discovered in Helsinki, the two female heads date from 1905. The self-portrait of the artist holding her hand to her forehead was made in June 1910. It is now believed that all the lithographs and etchings produced by the artist – more than 270 – have been identified.

" Her campaigning vision is a black tunnel of mourning. "

The Guardian, 2017

Lift Every Voice and Sing (The Harp)

Augusta Savage

1939

When the organizers of the 1939 New York World's Fair commissioned a piece from the sculptor Augusta Savage, she must have hoped that the work would be cast in bronze after the fair, sealing her reputation.

In 1934, Florida-born Savage became the first Black American to be elected to the National Association of Women Artists. She was also the only Black American woman commissioned to make a work for the 1939 New York exhibition. She was asked to create a piece that reflected Black American music. For inspiration, she turned to the poem *Lift Ev'ry Voice and Sing*, written in 1900 by James Weldon Johnson and set to music by his brother John. The anthem had gained popularity among Black Americans as a call for equality.

> **"** It was one of the most popular works in the fair, seen by over 5 million people. It's an extraordinary loss. **"**
>
> **Wendy N.E. Ikemoto**, exhibition curator, 2019

Augusta Savage working on *Lift Every Voice and Sing*

Lift Every Voice and Sing, which stood 4.9 m (16 ft) high, was composed of a line of 12 singers in decreasing height, suggesting the shape of a harp. An extended forearm supporting the singers formed the harp's sound board. Savage modelled it in plaster and painted it with a dark gloss paint to resemble bronze. Retitled *The Harp* by the fair's organizers, *Lift Every Voice and Sing* was positioned in the courtyard of the Pavilion of Contemporary Art, where it was seen by more than 5 million visitors. Metal replicas 28 cm (11 in) high were sold as souvenirs.

When the exhibition closed, Savage could not get financial support to cover the cost of casting the piece. Nor could she afford to store it. It was destroyed by workmen along with other artworks from the fair. *Lift Every Voice and Sing* was her last important exhibit.

In 2021, a decision was taken to make a copy of the original statue for Lift Ev'ry Voice and Sing Park, which was being created at 120 Lee Street, Jacksonville, Florida, where the Johnson brothers were born, and near Savage's birthplace in Green Cove Springs.

Portrait of
Winston Churchill

⟡

Graham Sutherland

1954

Winston Churchill at the unveiling of the portrait painted by
Graham Sutherland

When the British Houses of Parliament presented the Prime Minister, Sir Winston Churchill, with a portrait to mark his 80th birthday on 30 November 1954, the politician was far from pleased. At a televised ceremony in Westminster Hall, he hid his hatred of the painting by describing it as "a remarkable example of modern art". The original intention was that the portrait would be hung at Westminster after Churchill's death.

> ❝ He felt he had been betrayed by the artist, whom he had liked ... he found in the portrait causes for moral affront. ❞
>
> **Mary Soames**, Churchill's youngest daughter

Churchill's wife, Lady Clementine, saw the finished portrait by the British painter Graham Sutherland in advance of the ceremony, and appeared to like it. But when she showed Churchill a photograph of the work, he threatened not to attend the unveiling ceremony, claiming that the portrait represented an old man in a nursing home. He described it as "malignant" and "filthy". Only with difficulty was the irascible prime minister persuaded that it would be an insult to the donors to boycott the festivities. A few days before the presentation, Churchill wrote to Sutherland complaining that the portrait was not a realistic rendering. To this, Sutherland politely replied that it was how he perceived the Prime Minister.

After the ceremony, Sutherland's portrait was sent to the Churchills' home at Chartwell, in Kent, and was not seen again. The year after Lady Churchill's death in 1977, it transpired that she had arranged for the painting to be destroyed within a year or two of the presentation so that her husband would not be annoyed by it any longer.

Figurative Work

―――――◆―――――

Wu Guanzhong

1950s–1966

When Chinese artist Wu Guanzhong died in 2010, at the age of 90, he left a large body of work and was considered one of China's greatest modern artists. But his career is overshadowed by the painful memory of a group of paintings that he created when young, and later destroyed with his own hands.

Having graduated from China's National Academy of Fine Arts, Wu won a place at the École Nationale Supérieure des Beaux-Arts in Paris, where he studied between 1947 and 1950. This seminal period allowed him to visit the great galleries and museums of the French capital, and study work by Vincent van Gogh, Pablo Picasso, and the French Impressionists.

Wu returned home to find the Chinese Democratic Socialist Party in power. Artists were required to concentrate on socialist realist themes of heroic soldiers and workers. Knowing this did not suit his own European-influenced style, Wu turned to landscape painting and teaching.

When Mao Zedong launched the Cultural Revolution, a brutal purge of "class enemies", in 1966, Wu feared the authorities would condemn his work, so he destroyed most of his paintings, including several nudes, from his time in Paris. He was right to be worried. That year, he was forbidden to paint or teach art and was sent to work on a farm. After six years, Wu was permitted to paint murals in public buildings as long as he followed government guidelines.

When the political situation eased after the death of Mao in 1976, Wu re-emerged on the artistic scene, producing landscapes that combined the lightness of China's traditional pen-and-ink calligraphy with the bright colours of Western oil painting. But he would never be able to replace the works he had destroyed.

Reclining Figure

Henry Moore
1969–70

The theft of a huge bronze statue made by the English sculptor Henry Moore on a dark December night in 2005 may have had more to do with the price of precious metals than with the art market. The 2-tonne (4,000-lb), 3.6-m- (111-ft-) long *Reclining Nude* (1969), worth £3 million, is suspected to have been cut into pieces and sold abroad for scrap, possibly for as little as £1,500. It is unclear whether this was a robbery gone wrong, requiring the thieves to dispose of the evidence, or whether the statue was stolen purely for its scrap-metal value.

Moore cast an edition of six bronze *Reclining Nudes* for sale, and kept a seventh in his own collection at Perry Green in Hertfordshire. It was this one that attracted the nocturnal thieves, who drove into the estate with a pick-up lorry and lifting equipment. There was no security as the sculptures were thought to be too big and heavy to be stolen. Although the police favour the scrap-metal motive, it is likely that professional thieves would have known that Moore's work regularly sells for millions of pounds. As a result, the file remains open in the hope that the thieves may have sold the statue to an art collector, from whose collection it might one day emerge.

Everyone I Have Ever Slept With

Tracey Emin

1995

" [The tent]'s a seminal thing. It was that moment and that time in my life. It's me sitting in my flat in Waterloo sewing all the names on. "

Tracey Emin, 2004

A t 3.43 am on 24 May 2004, London's Leyton Fire Station received an emergency call alerting it to a vast fire at an East London industrial estate. As intruders had left the premises of an electrical goods storage company, they had set the building on fire, by either accident or design.

What had begun as just another London burglary escalated into the largest conflagration of modern British art. The flames quickly spread to a warehouse leased by Momart, a British company that specializes in the storage of fine art. The building was rapidly engulfed in flames, and despite the efforts of the fire brigade, it was entirely destroyed within a few hours. The area was so severely damaged that police were unable to begin investigating the site for five days. Several units adjacent to the smouldering ruins contained flammable substances and these had to be secured before fire fighters entered the site. By this time, nothing could be salvaged from the inferno.

Momart had an impressive list of clients, including major galleries and leading collectors and artists. Charles Saatchi lost around 100 pieces from his collection of Young British Artists. Damien Hirst lost several of his own works and ones he owned by other artists. Fifty canvases by the British painter Patrick Heron were destroyed. Other artists to lose work included Paula Rego, Gillian Ayres, and Chris Ofili.

One of the highest profile pieces to burn was Tracey Emin's *Everyone I Have Ever Slept With 1963–1995* (*The Tent*) (1995), a tent appliquéd with the names of 102 of her acquaintances, lovers, family, and friends, which had been bought by Saatchi for £40,000. Another piece, also in the Saatchi collection, was the Chapman brothers' *Hell* (2000), a series of glass cases in which thousands of miniature model Nazi soldiers were being tortured and killed in a disturbing comment on the horrors of genocide. Emin refused to consider making a copy of *The Tent*, even though it would have allowed her to update the work with new names. She said, "I couldn't remake that time in my life any more than I could remake the piece." By contrast, Jake and Dinos Chapman recreated and expanded *Hell*, producing several new versions.

While some works could have been recreated, the thorny issue of loss of earnings remained. Would a remade work have the value of the original? Who would compensate the artists and owners for loss of earnings from future exhibitions and potential sales? Artists, galleries, auction houses, and collectors tried to win compensation from Momart. They finally took the firm to court, claiming that its security had been inadequate and insufficient fire detection and prevention systems had been installed. Momart counter-argued that clients were obliged to have their own insurance.

In 2007, the case was settled out of court for a reported sum of tens of millions of pounds. There is no way of calculating how much the destroyed art was worth, but estimates range from £30 million to £50 million.

Paint attack

When *The Holy Virgin Mary* (1996) by the Turner-Prize winning British artist Chris Ofili (left), went on display at New York's Brooklyn Museum of Art in December 1999, it created heated debate. A local resident, Dennis Heiner, took offence at the portrait, which included cut-outs from pornographic magazines and elephant dung, and smeared it with white latex paint. He was charged with defacement and fined $250. The work was cleaned and put back on display.

" No one died and
ideas continue. "

Tracey Emin, 2004

EVERYONE I HAVE EVER SLEPT WITH

Tracey Emin, 2004

Dropping a Han Dynasty Urn

———◇———

Ai Weiwei

1995

In 1995, Chinese artist Ai Weiwei posed for a sequence of three photographs of himself holding and then deliberately dropping a Han dynasty urn that was more than 2,000 years old. The artist later described this as a subversive and transformative act. He said, "The images depicted a stoic young man committing an act of destruction, or creation, upon an ancient vessel." He had asked his brother to take the photographs in order to test a new Nikon camera. It was the second urn he had smashed, as his brother had failed to capture the act on his first attempt.

Since returning to China from the US in 1993, Ai Weiwei had been exploring how ancient Chinese artefacts reflected the period of history in which they were made, while also influencing the country's aesthetics and culture. He had bought various ancient items very cheaply in the country's antiquities markets, and had incorporated them into his artwork in new and provocative ways.

> " It's powerful only because
> someone thinks it's powerful
> and invests value in the object. "
>
> **Ai Weiwei**

Ai Weiwei did not originally consider the sequence of photographs to be an artwork. He included it in *The White Cover Book*, a platform for work by underground Chinese artists, which was published in 1995, but it did not receive a wide audience until 2006, when it was included in his first exhibition, at Queensland Art Gallery in Australia. Critical reception was mixed. Some condemned the wilful destruction of an ancient artefact, while others lauded it as an act of creative genius.

Ai Weiwei's *Dropping a Han Dynasty Urn* (1995)

In 2014, Florida-based artist Maximo Caminero carried out a copycat act while attending Ai Weiwei's *According to What?* exhibition at the Pérez Art Museum in Miami. While looking at *Dropping A Han Dynasty Urn* on the gallery wall, Caminero picked up a pot from the adjacent display, a set of ancient urns that Ai Weiwei had painted in bright colours. He then dropped the pot, in imitation of Ai Weiwei.

Caminero's action was not greeted as a burst of genius. Instead, he was arrested and charged for smashing an artwork that was worth more than $1 million. Caminero argued that he had smashed Ai Weiwei's work in a spontaneous act as a means of getting attention for Miami-based artists squeezed out by the focus on international artists. He said, "When you visit a city and go to its museums you want to see what that city has to offer. You don't come to Miami to see Van Gogh or Picasso."

Pillar
of Shame

Jens Galschiøt

1996

Pillar of Shame before it was dismantled and removed.

In 1996, Danish artist Jens Galschiøt sculpted a monument to the protesters who had been killed in pro-democracy protests in Beijing's Tiananmen Square on 4 June 1989. Thousands of students had gathered in Tiananmen Square, demanding increased political freedoms. Afraid it could lose its grip on power, the Chinese government had sent in the army to break up the protest. Tanks and troops had opened fire on the protesters, shooting indiscriminately at the unarmed students. Estimates of the number killed vary from hundreds to 10,000.

Galschiøt's copper sculpture, called *Pillar of Shame or Martyr's Monument*, stood 8 m (26 ft) tall and consisted of a thin column of broken and twisting human bodies. It was installed in Hong Kong's Victoria Park to mark the eighth anniversary of the massacre and then moved to the University of Hong Kong campus.

Several memorials to the Tiananmen Square protesters were erected in Hong Kong, but by 2021 most of them had been removed. An annual candlelit vigil marking the episode was also banned in 2020 and 2021, supposedly due to concerns over the Covid virus. Then, in October 2021, the University of Hong Kong requested that the *Pillar of Shame* also be removed. No reason was provided.

Galschiøt appealed to the university authorities, asking them to return the work to him if they wanted to remove it from public view. Over the next few weeks, students tried to protect the statue, but on 22 December, while students were away on a break, a removal crew moved in. Surrounding the memorial with a screen of plastic sheeting so no one could see what was happening, and under the cover of darkness, they dismantled the monument and took it away in pieces. In the next few days, two more universities removed Tiananmen Square memorials from their campuses.

" A very hard attack against the free word in the world. "

Jens Galschiøt

Love is in the Bin

Banksy

2018

On 5 October 2018, an ink drawing titled *Girl with a Balloon* (2006) by the British graffiti artist Banksy sold at Sotheby's auction house in London for the record price of £1,042,000. But after the gavel fell, bidders watched as the drawing slowly slid down through a miniature shredder that the artist had inserted into the bottom edge of the gilt frame. Within a few seconds, the mechanism stopped, leaving the lower portion of the drawing in shreds. The shredder had been operated remotely, and the artist later declared that the hidden mechanism had been inserted to prevent resale, and that the semi-destroyed work was now fully complete. He retitled it *Love Is in the Bin*.

At first, the shocked buyer rejected the purchase, but was convinced by a Sotheby's specialist that the bizarre process would increase the value of the work. The buyer reluctantly completed

The canvas passes through a hidden shredder, Sotheby's auction room, 2018

" I can't tell you how terrified I am to bring down this hammer. "

Oliver Barker, Sotheby's, 2018

the transfer of the funds six days later. But the specialist's prediction proved correct. When the half-shredded work came up for auction once more at Sotheby's, on 14 October 2021, it sold for £18,582,000, an auction record for the artist.

Love is in the Bin belongs to a rich history of art that questions the value placed on it, from French painter and sculptor Marcel Duchamp's iconic *Fountain* (1917), a standard urinal bought from a sanitary manufacturer, to Ai Weiwei's *Dropping a Han Dynasty Urn* (see page 182), three photographs of the artist doing exactly that.

Index

A

Abstract Expressionism 54
Academy of Science, Almaty 55
Accademia Gallery, Venice 28
Adam and Eve (George Petel)
  78–79
Adoration of the Mystic Lamb see
  Ghent Altarpiece
Ai Weiwei 182–183, 187
al-Idrisi 22–23
Alexander Mosaic 18–19
Alexander the Great 18–19
altarpieces 62–65
Altmann, Maria 98–99
Amber Room 154–155
American War for Independence
  163
Ancient Egyptian artefacts 10–13
Anglo-Saxon artefacts 121
Anna Feodorovna (Elisabeth Vigée
  Le Brun) 34–35
Aphrodite of Knidos (Praxiteles)
  14–15
Ayres, Gillian 170, 179
Azevedo, Néle 57

B

Bacon, Francis 106
Bandini Pietà (Michelangelo)
  130–131
Banksy 186–187
Basquiat, Jean-Michel 108
Battle of Hastings 124
Battle of Issus 19
The Battle of San Jacinto (Henry
  Arthur McArdle) 40
Bayeux Museum 125
Bayeux Tapestry 124–125
Beechey, William 153
Beltracchi, Wolfgang 43
Benin Bronzes 70–73
Bern Historical Museum 147

Bieslijn, Henk 92
Bloch-Bauer, Ferdinand and Adele
  98, 99
The Blue Room (Picasso) 164–165
Bodleian Library, Oxford 23
Boltraffio, Giovanni 26
Bonfire of the Vanities 148–149
Book of the Dead 13
Book of Kells 61
Botticelli, Sandro 103, 148
Bouts, Dieric 69
Breitwieser, Stéphane 79
British Museum 15, 73, 119, 120
Brooklyn Museum of Art 180
Bruegel, Pieter, the Elder 85
Buddhas of Bamiyan 144–145

C

Ca' d'Oro, Venice 28
Cambridge, Robert 130
Camille Claudel Museum,
  Nogent-sur-Seine 94
Caminero, Maximo 183
Camouflage Series (Andy Warhol)
  109
Campbell's Soup Cans (Andy
  Warhol) 109
Canova, Antonio 57
Capital Museum, Beijing 33
Caravaggio 74–75
Carter, Howard 10, 11, 13
cartography 22–23
Cassatt, Mary 38–39
Castiglione, Giuseppe 32
Catherine Palace 154–155
Chagall, Marc 100
Chapman, Jake and Dinos 180
Charing Cross Bridge, London
  (Claude Monet) 104
Chez Tortoni (Édouard Manet) 81
Chloe & Emma (Barbora Kysilkova)
  110–111

*Christ in the Storm on the Sea of
  Galilee* (Rembrandt van Rijn)
  81, 82
Churchill, Winston 174–175
Claudel, Camille 94–95
Cleveland Museum of Art 122–123
The Concert (Johannes Vermeer)
  80, 83
*Congregation Leaving the Reformed
  Church in Nuenen* (Vincent van
  Gogh) 92–93
Corot, Jean-Baptiste-Camille 85
Courbet, Gustave 85, 160–161
Cracked Canyon (Valerie Hegarty)
  141
Cultural Revolution 176, 182

D

Darius III of Persia 19
Daumier, Honoré 85
David, Jacques-Louis 156–157
De Haan, Meyer 104
De Lempicka, Tamara 105
The Death of Cleopatra (Edmonia
  Lewis) 36–37
The Death of Marat (Jacques-Louis
  David) 157
December in Venice (Charles
  Polowetski) 44–45
Degas, Edgar 39, 81, 86–87
"Degenerate Art" exhibition
  100, 101
Delacroix, Eugène 84–85
Diyabanza, Emery Mwazulu
  88, 89
Dogaru, Olga and Radu 104
The Dream (Pablo Picasso) 136–137
Dropping a Han Dynasty Urn (Ai
  Weiwei) 182–183, 187
Duchamp, Marcel 187
Dürer, Albrecht 147, 150
Durham, Octave 92

E

Edo Museum of West African Art, Benin City 73
El Greco 150
Elgin, Lord 118
Emin, Tracey 178–181
Emperor Charles V at Mühlberg (Titian) 153
ephemeral works 57
Equestrian Portrait of Emperor Philip IV (Peter Paul Rubens) 150, 153
Everyone I Have Ever Slept With (Tracey Emin) 178–181
The Expulsion of the Moriscos (Diego Velázquez) 150

F

Federal Art Project (FAP) 45
Flinck, Govaert 81
Fogerty, William 90
Fondaco dei Tedeschi, Venice 28
forgeries 42–43
Fountain (Marcel Duchamp) 187
French Revolution 34, 157
frescoes 28, 126–127
Freud, Lucian 104, 106
Frida Kahlo Museum, Baden-Baden 49
funerary pole 88

G

Gainsborough, Thomas 76, 85
Galleri Nobel, Oslo 110
Galschiøt, Jens 184–185
García, Ramón Sardina 60
The Gates of Hell (Auguste Rodin and Camille Claudel) 94–95
Gauguin, Paul 104
Gentileschi, Artemisia 30–31
George III Reviewing the Troops (William Beechey) 153
Ghent Altarpiece (Jan and Hubert van Eyck) 62–63, 101–102
Giorgione 28
Giotto di Bondone 127
Girl with a Balloon (Banksy) 186

Girl in Front of Open Window (Paul Gauguin) 104
Goebbels, Joseph 101
The Golden Legend (Jacobus de Voraigne) 69
Golden Lyre of Ur 117
Goldsworthy, Andy 56–57
Gori, Vittorio Cecchi 108
Göring, Hermann 101
Goya, Francisco 76
Grand Egyptian Museum, Giza 13, 73
Guardi, Francesco 76
Gurlitt, Cornelius 103
Gurlitt, Hildebrand 100

H

Han Dynasty 182
Harlequin Head (Pablo Picasso) 104
The Head of a Bearded Man (Peter Paul Rubens) 76–77
Hegarty, Valerie 140–141
Hell (Jake and Dinos Chapman) 180
Hepworth, Barbara 107
Heron, Patrick 179
Hill, Charles 96–97
Hirst, Damien 179
Hitler, Adolf 101
Hogan, Paul 90
The Holy Virgin Mary (Chris Ofili) 180
Hugh Lane Gallery, Dublin 90

I

illuminated manuscripts 61
Imperiale, Raffaele 92
The Invisible Enemy Should Not Exist (Michael Rakowitz) 116
Irish Republican Army (IRA) 76
Isabella Stewart Gardner Museum, Boston 80–83
Islamic State (ISIS) 114, 116

J

J. Paul Getty Museum, California 30
Jesus College, Cambridge 73

Johnson, James Weldon and John Rosamond 172, 173
The Justice of Trajan and Herkinbald (Rogier van der Weyden) 146–147

K

Kahlo, Frida 48–49
Kandinsky, Wassily 100
Kauffman, Angelica 158–159
Klee, Paul 100, 102, 103
Klimt, Gustav 98–99
Kollwitz, Käthe 170–171
Kunsthal, Rotterdam 104
Kusama, Yayoi 138–139
Kysilkova, Barbora 110–111

L

A Lady and Gentleman in Black (Rembrandt van Rijn) 81
lamassu (mythical beasts) 114–117
Landscape with Obelisk (Govaert Flinck) 81
Lane, Hugh 90–91
Las Meninas (Diego Velázquez) 153
The Last Judgement (Hans Memling) 64–65
The Last Moments of Michel Lepeletier (Jacques-Louis David) 156–157
Lawrence, Jacob 50–51
Lenin, Vladimir 55, 168–169
Lenin mosaic 55
Leonardo da Vinci 24–27, 66–67, 103, 130, 150
Lepeletier, Louis-Michel 157
Les Choristes (Edgar Degas) 86–87
Leutze, Emanuel Gottlieb 162–163
Levine, Josh 54
Lewis, Edmonia 36–37
Liebermann, Max 100
Life of St Francis (Giotto) 127
Lift Every Voice and Sing (Augusta Savage) 172–173
Lioness and Lion in a Cave (Eugène Delacroix) 84–85

Louvre, Paris 15, 67, 69
Love, Iris Cornelia 15
Love Is in the Bin (Banksy) 186–187
Lucretia (Artemisia Gentileschi)
  30–31
Lundens, Gerrit 133

M

McArdle, Henry Arthur 40
Madonna (Edvard Munch) 97
Madonna and Child (Michelangelo)
  102
Maier, Vivian 52–53
Man at the Crossroads (Diego
  Rivera) 168–169
Manet, Édouard 39, 81
Marat, Jean-Paul 157
Martini, Simone 127
Matisse, Henri 100, 104
Mayan artefacts 60
Melting Man (Néle Azevedo) 57
Memling, Hans 64–65, 69
Mesopotamian art 114–117
Metropolitan Museum of Art,
  New York 13, 50, 51, 163
Michelangelo 102, 128–131
Mexican antiquities 60
Mills Mansion, Mount Morris
  44, 45
Miró, Joan 46–47
Modern Woman (Mary Cassatt)
  38–39
Modigliani, Amedeo 42–43
Momart 179, 180
Mona Lisa (Leonardo da Vinci)
  66–67
Monet, Claude 100, 104, 166–167
Montreal Museum of Fine Arts
  84–85
monumental public art 55
Monuments, Fine Arts, and Archives
  Program 102, 103
Monuments Men 103
Moore, Henry 177
Morisot, Berthe 90–91
mosaics 18–19, 55
Mulcahy, William 120

Munch, Edvard 96–97
murals 39, 46–47, 168–169
Museum of Anthropology, Mexico
  City 60
Museum of Black Civilizations,
  Senegal 73
Museum of Humankind, Kenya
  73
Museum of Maritime History,
  Mozambique 73
Museum of Modern Art, New York
  166–167
Myrto (Tamara de Lempicka) 105

N

National Archaeological Museum,
  Naples 19
National Gallery, London 130, 134,
  135, 159
National Gallery of Ireland, Dublin
  76
National Museum of Cambodia
  122–123
National Museum of China 33
National Museum of Iraq 117
*Nativity with St Francis and St
  Lawrence* (Caravaggio) 74–75
Nazism 100–102
Niagara Falls (Valerie Hegarty)
  140–141
The Night Watch (Rembrandt van
  Rijn) 132–133
Nimrod 114
Nineveh 114–117
Nordland, Karl-Bertil 110–111

O

Ofili, Chris 179, 180
O'Keeffe, Georgia 41
Opera del Duomo, Florence 131

P

Palais de Lomé, Togo 73
Palmyra 116
Pan African Heritage World
  Museum, Ghana 73
Parthenon Marbles 118–119

Peruggia, Vincenzo 67
Petel, George 78–79
pharaohs 10–13
Phidias 118
Philadelphia Museum of Art 69
Picasso, Pablo 100, 104, 136–137,
  164–165
Pietà (Michelangelo) 128–130
Pillar of Shame (Jens Galschiøt)
  184–185
Pollock, Jackson 54
Polowetski, Charles 44–45
Poly Art Museum, Beijing 33
Pompeii 19
Pop Art 109
Portland Vase 120
Portraits of Adele (Gustav Klimt)
  98–99
Praxiteles 15
Ptolemy 22
Pushkin Museum, Moscow 34

Q

Qin Shi Huang, Emperor 16
Quai Branly Museum, Paris 88

R

Raedwald 121
Rakowitz, Michael 116
Raphael 29, 150
Reading Girl in White and Yellow
  (Henri Matisse) 104
The Reaper (Joan Miró) 46–47
Reclining Nude (Amedeo Modigliani)
  42–43
Reclining Figure (Henry Moore)
  177
Red and Green II (Georgia O'Keeffe)
  41
Ree, Benjamin 111
Rego, Paula 179
Religion Attended by the Virtues
  (Angelica Kauffman) 158–159
Rembrandt van Rijn 40, 81, 103,
  132–133
restitution of art works 13, 73,
  88–89, 98–99, 102–103, 119

Richardson, Mary 134–135
Rijksmuseum, Amsterdam 133
Rivera, Diego 49, 168–169
Rockefeller, Nelson 166, 168, 169
Rodin, Auguste 94–95
Roger II of Sicily 22, 23
The Rokeby Venus (Diego Velázquez) 134–135
Royal Academy of Arts 158
Royal Alcázar, Madrid 150–153
Rubens, Peter Paul 76–77, 79, 85, 150, 151, 153
Rubens House Museum, Antwerp 79
Russborough House 76

S

Saatchi, Charles 179, 180
St Bavo's Cathedral, Ghent 62
St Christopher Carrying the Christ Child (Jan van Eyck) 68–69
St Francis of Assisi 127
St Peter's Basilica, Rome 128, 130
Salvator Mundi (Leonardo da Vinci) 24–27
Savage, Augusta 172–173
Savonarola, Girolomo 148, 149
The Scream (Edvard Munch) 96–97
Self-portrait with Hand on Forehead (Käthe Kollwitz) 171
Self-Portrait (Meyer de Haan) 104
Shawcross, Conrad 107
Sistine tapestries 29
Smithsonian, Washington, D.C. 37
Solari, Cristoforo 130
Spanish Civil War 46
Stoclet, Adolphe 122
The Stone Breakers (Gustave Courbet) 160–161
street photography 52–53
Struggle: From the History of the American People (Jacob Lawrence) 50–51
Suffragettes 135
Summer's Day (Berthe Morisot) 90–91

Sutherland, Graham 174–175
Sutton Hoo Helmet 121
Swamp Legend (Paul Klee) 100, 102, 103
Swan Song (Barbora Kysilkova) 110

T

Tabula Rogeriana (al-Idrisi) 22–23
Taliban 144–145
Tang Dynasty 20
tapestries 29, 124–125, 147
Tate Gallery, London 90, 106, 159
Terracotta Army 16–17
Three Perpetual Chords (Conrad Shawcross) 107
Tiananmen Square pro-democracy protests 185
Tintoretto 150
Titian 28, 150, 153
tomb-raiders 10, 20
Toth, Lazlo 128, 129
Touching North (Andy Goldsworthy) 56–57
Treviño, Carlos Perches 60
Trinity College Library, Dublin 61
Tutankhamun, tomb of 10–13
Tverdokhlebov, Vladimir 55
Two Forms (Divided Circle) (Barbara Hepworth) 107

U

Uffizi Galleries, Florence 153
Unconscious Patient (Allegory of Smell) (Rembrandt van Rijn) 40

V

Valley of the Kings 10
Van der Weyden, Rogier 146–147
Van Eyck, Hubert 62–63
Van Eyck, Jan 62–63, 68–69
Van Gogh, Vincent 92–93
Van Gogh Museum, Amsterdam 92–93
Vasari, Giorgio 69, 130
Velázquez, Diego 134–135, 150, 153

Venus and Adonis (Diego Velázquez) 150
Vermeer, Johannes 76, 80, 83, 103
Veronese, Paolo 150
Vesuvius, Mount 19
View of the Sea at Scheveningen (Vincent van Gogh) 92–93
Vigée Le Brun, Elisabeth 34–35
The Virgin and Child with St Anne and St John the Baptist (Leonardo da Vinci) 130
Vishnu, statue of 122–123

W

The Waltz (Camille Claudel) 94
Warhol, Andy 109
Warka Vase 117
Washington Crossing the Delaware (Emanuel Gottlieb Leutze) 162–163
Washington Principles 103
Water Lilies (Claude Monet) 166–167
Waterloo Bridge, London (Claude Monet) 104
Wedgwood, Josiah 120
Windsor Castle 153
Wine of Babylon (Jean-Michel Basquiat) 108
Woman with Eyes Closed (Lucien Freud) 104
World War II 34, 62, 65, 98, 101, 103, 105, 154, 155, 159, 160
The Wounded Table (Frida Kahlo) 48–49
Wu Guanzhong 176
Wynn, Steve 136–137

Y

Yellow Pumpkin (Yayoi Kusama) 138–139

Z

zhenmoushou (guardian beasts) 20–21
Zodiac Fountain Water Clock 32–33

Acknowledgments

Toucan Books

Editorial Director Ellen Dupont; **Editors** Helen Douglas-Cooper, Dorothy Stannard; **Designer** Dave Jones; **Consultant** Aliki Braine; **Picture Researcher** Sharon Southren; **Researcher** Benjamin Hartnell-Booth; **Authenticity Readers** Stephanie Cohen, Kit Heyam, Nancy Tolson; **Proofreader** Julie Brooke; **Indexer** Marie Lorimer